the series on school reform

Ann Lieberman, *Senior Scholar, Stanford University*   Joseph P. McDonald, *New York University*
SERIES EDITORS

(Continued)

the series on school reform, *continued*

The Mindful Teacher

SECOND EDITION

Dennis Shirley
Elizabeth MacDonald

TEACHERS COLLEGE PRESS

TEACHERS COLLEGE | COLUMBIA UNIVERSITY
NEW YORK AND LONDON

Published by Teachers College Press, 1234 Amsterdam Avenue, New York, NY
10027

Library of Congress Cataloging-in-Publication Data

Names: Shirley, Dennis, 1955– author. | MacDonald, Elizabeth, 1973– author.
Title: The mindful teacher / Dennis Shirley and Elizabeth MacDonald.
Description: Second edition. | New York, NY : Teachers College Press, [2016]
  | Series: The series on school reform | Previous edition entered under:
  MacDonald, Elizabeth, 1973– | Includes bibliographical references and
  index.
Identifiers: LCCN 2016012416 (print) | LCCN 2016017071 (ebook) | ISBN
  9780807756843 (pbk.) | ISBN 9780807772522 (ebook)
Subjects: LCSH: Reflective teaching. | Buddhism and education. |
  Teaching—Psychological aspects.
Classification: LCC LB1027.22 .M34 2016 (print) | LCC LB1027.22 (ebook) | DDC
  371.102—dc23
LC record available at https://lccn.loc.gov/2016012416

ISBN 978-0-8077-5684-3 (paper)
ISBN 978-0-8077-7252-2 (ebook)

Printed on acid-free paper

Manufactured in the United States of America

23 22 21 20 19 18 17 16   8 7 6 5 4 3 2 1

Dedicated with Gratitude
To Our Teachers

To affect the quality of the day, that is the highest of arts.

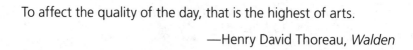

—Henry David Thoreau, *Walden*

Contents

Acknowledgments

Our first thanks go to the philanthropists and selection committee members of the Boston Collaborative Fellows Grant. This innovative grant encourages professors in the Lynch School of Education at Boston College to conduct collaborative research with their colleagues in the Boston Public Schools. Without the generous support of this grant the Mindful Teacher project would not have been possible.

This project also benefited from support from several other foundations and centers that have supported one or both of us. These include the Rockefeller Foundation's Study and Conference Center in Bellagio, Italy; the Alexander von Humboldt Foundation in Bonn, Germany; the Freudenberg Foundation in Weinheim, Germany; the Scholars' Forum of the Public Education Network in Washington, D.C.; and the Carnegie Corporation's Teachers for a New Era project, based in New York City.

We are indebted to many educators who have explored with us the principles and practices of mindful teaching. In the United States, the Arizona K12 Center has been a steadfast supporter. In Singapore, we are indebted to the National Institute of Education at Nanyang Technological University for its invitations. We have learned much from our presentations at events sponsored by the Australian Council for Educational Research, the Australian Council of Educational Leaders, the German School Academy, the Union of Educators Norway, the Research Council of Norway, the Alberta Teachers' Association, and the Council of Ontario Directors of Education in Canada.

Sections of Chapter 6 previously appeared in "The Fourth Way of Technology and Change," by Dennis Shirley, 2011, *Journal of Educational Change*, 12(2), 187–209.

The Mindful Teacher

Introduction
The Quiet Revolution

When the first edition of *The Mindful Teacher* was published in 2009, the concept of "mindfulness" was just beginning to work its way into schools. At the time, few schools had offerings for their students in contemplative practices, and even the notion of quiet or restorative time for educators and their students was anathema. A reform movement pushing higher standards, more testing, more accountability, more markets, and more technology was in full force.

How things change! By 2016 the old reform imperatives had exhausted themselves. In the United States, the passage of the Every Student Succeeds Act overturned many of the prescriptive policies of the ill-fated No Child Left Behind Act. The high-achieving educational system in Singapore had implemented a new policy of "Teach Less, Learn More" that preserved 10% of classroom time as "white space" for educators to step outside of mandated curricula and come up with their own projects based on student interests (Hargreaves & Shirley, 2012). Ontario, Canada, which also has a world-leading system, had expanded its educational goals to include student well-being as one of its top four priorities (Ontario Ministry of Education, 2014). Overall, researchers found that when students use guided meditation practices to calm their bodies and focus their minds, their learning and self-regulation improve compared with control groups (Rechtschaffen, 2014). A cottage industry of mindfulness offerings was growing in popularity in schools and society, revealing enthusiasm for a values-oriented and caring curriculum.

What does it all mean? A *quiet revolution* is beginning to spread around the world to enable schools to attain their potential to become places of learning and joy. This quiet revolution welcomes *all* students: the rich and the poor, the brilliant and the struggling, females

1

and males, those who are just trying to fit in and those who want to stand out. Students, parents, and educators are indicating that they want to restore the grandeur of teaching and learning as enterprises befitting the dignity of the young and the moral purpose of the adults. Keywords such as pressure, standards, markets, accountability, technology, and testing that have commanded attention as elixirs and panaceas for the past quarter century have lost their force. We are witnessing the gradual, iterative, painstaking emergence of new ideas and practices. These emphasize balance, well-being, sustainability, and integrity, and are distilled into one overarching term: *mindfulness*.

This slowly emerging cultural evolution to a deeper form of educational inquiry has been years in the making. Ellen Langer, a Harvard psychologist, made mindfulness the topic of bestselling books (1989, 1997). Spiritual guides as diverse as Martin Luther King, Dorothy Day, Thomas Merton, Desmond Tutu, and Thich Nhat Hanh have emphasized different kinds of mindful discernment through their teachings. These leaders combined their passion for social justice with compassion for all living beings, including those who opposed them on parts of their agendas. Their cosmopolitan humanism taught us to look beyond the particular interests of one group to the overall improvement of the human condition. However it is defined and manifested, it seems that there is an almost insatiable desire for such forms of mindful teaching and learning at this historical moment.

And why not? Scholars in the field of "subjective well-being" can produce mountains of data documenting that our fast-paced, stretched-thin lifestyles are correlated with a soaring rise in depression and a loss of locus of control (Lane, 2000; Seligman, 2002). Although the greatest determinant of our happiness has to do with the quality of our interpersonal relationships, advertising perpetually tries to persuade us that our greatest pleasures are to be found in consumption—and we all too often act as if this were true, sacrificing our relationships with friends and family in pursuit of material gratification. The recent economic crisis is only one manifestation of a larger crisis of values that has now reached virtually every corner of the globe. Small wonder that "mindfulness" is attractive to people who are looking for some deeper meaning in their lives, yet who are reluctant to give themselves over to forms of group membership that appear to mitigate against critical thinking and individualism.

As mindfulness teaching and learning slowly work their way into schools, they transform recent practices and policies. The old policy imperative to practice data-driven decision making led many educators to believe that they were drowning in the wrong kinds of data—the kind that not only shamed struggling schools, but were processed and returned to schools by testing agencies too late to have any instructional value for the individual pupils who were tested (Celio & Harvey, 2005; Ingram, Seashore Louis, & Schroeder, 2004). As a consequence of the "standards stampede" (Hargreaves, 2003, p. 176) of the past 25 years, teachers too often found themselves forced to keep up with district- and state-mandated "pacing guides" even when their students had not fully understood the material in the timeline indicated by the guides.

Educational leaders, working for years under pressure to meet No Child Left Behind's indicators, responded by telling teachers to focus on "bubble kids" who might bump a school's scores up above a given cut score—abandoning the traditional moral imperative of educators to teach *all* pupils (Booher-Jennings, 2005; Pedulla et al., 2003). Accountability was transformed into accountancy. Science turned into scientism. The legitimate aspiration for academic achievement was reduced to an obsession with test scores. What possibilities remained in the nooks and crannies of the profession for ethical, caring teachers to inspire their students with the sheer joy and delight that is to be found in learning?

ALIENATED TEACHING

This second edition of *The Mindful Teacher* explores this question with new and expanded materials, using the following approach. First, we describe what we conceptualize as "alienated teaching." From our perspective, alienated teaching has become endemic in far too many schools. In a nutshell, alienated teaching is that kind of teaching that teachers perform when they feel that they *must* comply with external conditions that they have not chosen and from which they inwardly dissent because the reforms do not serve their children well.

Alienated teaching has many different modalities that we map out in the pages that follow. In part, alienated teaching is a consequence of policy mandates at the district, state, and federal levels. In part, it is a result of educators' own (often unconscious) capitulation to cultural norms that undermined their own moral purpose and sense of efficacy. It is difficult to tease out just how much each of these components contributed to teachers' alienation. To do so, we begin with the following questions:

- How should teachers respond to standards-based reforms and the ways that reforms continually change, requiring shifts in their teaching?
- How should teachers act when curricular packages are prescribed that they feel certain will raise achievement results, but also know that there are important forms of learning that are not measured on standardized tests?
- How should teachers cope with the rhetoric of data-driven decision making that appears to negate the prosaic but nonetheless profoundly influential interactions that pupils have with their peers on a daily basis that can enhance or undermine learning?
- How can teachers even begin to focus on instruction when their pupils bring emotional issues from unstable home situations into the classroom that cry out for gentle reassurance from the one adult with whom they seem to have some stable and regular contact on a daily basis?

These kinds of questions have not been adequately addressed in teachers' professional development for years. Policymakers' fascinations with numbers and metrics translated into professional development focused on narrow forms of assessment without accompanying instructional assistance for educators. In the process, the complexities of students' lives outside of school—in all of their richness and diversity—were ignored. Education became more insular in the process, failing to explore the intersection between schools and society that lie at the foundation of democratic education (Dewey, 1916). In addition, a great deal of research on school improvement focused on issues of alignment between pedagogy, curricula, and assessment without acknowledging that in tumultuous policy environments, few schools (if any) enjoyed such alignment.

In one study by the RAND Corporation, a majority of elementary school teachers felt that math and science standards in their states "include more content than can be covered adequately in the school year" (Hamilton et al., 2007, p. 43). "In such a situation," the researchers noted, "teachers must decide on their own whether to cover some standards fully and omit others or whether to cover all the standards incompletely." In addition, significant minorities (on the order of 20–30%) of elementary teachers believed that the standards "do not cover some important content areas." The authors continued, "These teachers faced the dilemma of teaching the content though it was not included in the standards and would not be on the assessment or omitting the content though they believed it was important (Hamilton et al., 2007, p. 43).

Individual classroom teachers did not have the power to change the overall policy environment. Given the dilemmas that they faced, no amount of data could drive them to resolve these complicated decisions in ways that involve a complex variety of trade-offs, all of which have important ethical ramifications. But much of the dominant rhetoric of pupil achievement for years suggested that they should indeed be so driven, thereby extending and exacerbating the phenomenon of alienated teaching.

MINDFUL TEACHING

To overcome alienated teaching, we propose an alternative conception of mindful teaching, in which teachers struggle to attain congruence, integrity, and efficacy in their practice. Mindful teaching, in this account, is not a program that can be purchased, a recipe that can be followed, or a silver bullet that can be fired into your instruction to raise your test scores. Rather, it is a form of teaching that is informed by contemplative practices and teacher inquiry that enables teachers to interrupt their harried lifestyles, come to themselves through participation in a collegial community of inquiry and practice, and attend to aspects of their classroom instruction and pupils' learning that are ordinarily overlooked in the press of events.

As is the case with alienated teaching, mindful teaching can take a variety of forms. We explore these here not through prescription but through description and analysis. We draw upon diverse forms of our own work with educators to conceptualize and discuss the myriad challenges of teaching and how these can be addressed with efficacy and integrity.

As you read this book, we ask you to consider ideas and practices from your own classroom and school settings that manifest mindful teaching. Please do not think that these have to be big programmatic initiatives. They can and often do exist in the small, in-between spaces of our schools. We have abundant ways to get to know our students better before, during, and after classes. Mindful teaching invites us to pay attention to our students so that they can know that we care about them and want to do our utmost to prepare them for an unpredictable future.

Educators should not ask policymakers or administrators to tell us how to do this. This dimension of teaching—call it pastoral, interpersonal, spiritual, affective, or what you will—has drawn many of us into the profession. It is what makes our work meaningful, which in turn gives our lives meaning. This quest for meaning is an enormous resource. It keeps educators returning to our classrooms, week after week, month after month, and year after year.

THE MINDFUL TEACHER SEMINARS

From whence do we derive our data for our descriptions of alienated and mindful teaching? For years we have led seminars and workshops for educators entitled "The Mindful Teacher." These began 10 years ago with cohorts of urban public school teachers in Boston to inquire into their craft. Abandoning orthodox professional development structures and appropriating participatory research strategies that would provide multiple opportunities for teachers themselves to generate new findings (Cochran-Smith & Lytle, 1993, 2009), we determined at the outset that we would not articulate preestablished outcomes for the seminars and workshops. Rather, our goals were to establish maximum openness for teachers to identify and explore collaboratively what they experience as core dilemmas and problems in their practice, to address the whole host of issues that emerge in the urban environment that make it difficult for their pupils to excel, and to keep a fluid structure so that new topics could continually emerge and be taken up by our cohorts in ways that would advance their awareness and deepen their understanding of the complexities of teaching and learning.

Aware of the many barriers that have separated university from school-based faculty, we were determined to conduct collaborative research in which a classroom teacher and a higher education faculty member would take the lead. Classroom teachers themselves would play a major role in providing ideas and writing commentaries through a structure of "sustained interactivity" (Huberman, 1999) over years. The final product is the manifestation of our working together with colleagues and other settings. Although this collaboration began in Boston, it has since continued with educators in Australia, Canada, Chile, England, Germany, Norway, and Singapore. It has been augmented by a website, www.mindfulteacher.com, which is open to all.

THE PSYCHIC REWARDS OF TEACHING

Why did we initiate Mindful Teacher seminars in the first place? In large part, these seminars were catalyzed by a comment once made by a veteran urban educator who told a group of higher education faculty the following: "You at the university level have really good questions and do really good research, but *your* questions aren't *our* questions." If this remark is true—and countless conversations with teachers would seem to indicate that it does have a ring of truth to it—what *are* teachers' questions? Why is there such a great divide between teachers and researchers? Why is it so hard for teachers' questions to be asked in common activity settings, such as teachers' lounges, where teachers could pool their craft wisdom, come up with potential solutions, and then try out new strategies and evaluate them?

We suggest that it has to do with the strange culture of educational change that has been created in virtually all advanced industrialized nations. When one first enters teaching, one is excited by new opportunities that emerge. One learns of new district initiatives, often with outside philanthropic support, and eagerly pursues the earliest trainings to get ahead of the curve and to push forward with innovations. This can be a time of experimentation, adaptation, and genuine intellectual excitement (Evans, 2001).

Over time, however, as one becomes more experienced, one begins to note disturbing patterns. New superintendents arrive—on average every 3 years—with new curricular packages to implement and little knowledge of previous undertakings (Council of Great City Schools, 2014). Policymakers push reforms through central offices, often in the form of short 1- or 2-year grants that seem to come and go, with little understanding of the on-the-ground realities of real classrooms in real schools (Moore Johnson, Marietta, Higgins, Mapp, & Grossman, 2015). Teachers' own ideas and experiences often are overlooked, with greater acknowledgment awarded to more prestigious (and well-funded) outsiders (Stone-Johnson, 2015). In some schools with which we've worked, older curricula are actually locked up in closets so that teachers are forced to use new curricula. In other cases, old curricula are removed from the schools completely.

Few policymakers seem to understand that teachers are attracted to the profession primarily by its psychic rewards, and that top-down reforms need to be balanced with bottom-up creativity and initiative. Looking over the past quarter century of school reform, we see teachers who have been total-quality managed, shared-decision-making trained, outcomes-based-education restructured, computer-enhanced instructioned, and whole-school-improvement planned. Teachers have been readers and writers workshopped, constructivist-math investigated, and school and university partnered.

Is it any wonder that so many teachers have become weary of what change management scholar Eric Abrahamson (2004, p. 14) has described as "repetitive change syndrome"? Should anyone wonder that so many have decided to withdraw behind the closed doors of their classrooms, where they hone their craft in private?

THE UNHOLY TRINITY

The launching of the Mindful Teacher seminar was an effort for both of us to battle the kind of resignation that bedevils far too many experienced educators. Decades ago, sociologist Dan Lortie (1975) described teachers as caught up in an unholy trinity of conservatism, individualism, and presentism. In the uncertain environment of the classroom, teachers became conservative insofar as they clutched on to what worked and developed an intrinsic distaste for new reforms. They became individualistic because of the cellular nature of teaching and lack of opportunities to observe colleagues and to swap ideas. They fell prey to presentism because administrators failed to include them in long-term plans, so they simply focused on the day-to-day issues without being able to participate in the shaping of a broader common culture that could evolve over time.

Since Lortie's publication of *Schoolteacher: A Sociological Study*, teachers, researchers, and policymakers have endeavored to shake up the unholy trinity and to help teachers become more open to change, more collegial, and more active in the shaping of school cultures in not just the short term, but also the medium and long term. In many ways, these efforts have been successful, as teacher inquiry groups—alternately called professional learning communities, communities of learners, or teacher leadership teams—have proliferated (Lieberman & Miller, 2008; Stoll, Bolgam, McMahon, Wallace, & Thomas, 2006).

In the best cases, these kinds of new horizontal cultures in schools have provided teachers with support, enabled them to gain new ideas to incorporate into their classrooms, promoted a sense among teachers of being responsible for all of the children in the building (and not just those in their classes), and given them access to scholarship so that they can thoughtfully integrate new research findings into their longstanding repertoires of classroom activities (Bryk & Schneider, 2004; Lieberman & Wood, 2003; McLaughlin & Talbert, 2001; Newmann & Wehlage, 1995). A growing body of research, some of which is presented later in this book, indicates that when teachers expand their learning, pupil learning does indeed benefit (Chen, Heritage, & Lee, 2005; Hargreaves, Shirley, Evans, Stone-Johnson, & Riseman, 2007; Symonds, 2003).

In other cases, even the best reforms became tainted (McQuillan, 1998; Payne, 2008). Rather than providing teachers with resources for meaningful collaboration, in some instances educational leaders mandated structural reforms without accompanying attention to culture, creating a kind of "contrived collegiality" that reinforced teacher cynicism (Hargreaves, 1994, p. 186). The openness that appeared to be promised through teacher collaboration too often became captive to the drive to increase pupil test scores (Hargreaves & Shirley, 2009a). The concerns of teachers who had other issues—what to do with a child whose mother was a crack addict and who attended school irregularly; how to defuse a conflict between two boys that seemed to escalate with clockwork regularity into a fight every Friday after lunch; or how to encourage children to develop their own curricular themes and interests—were viewed as distractions to the tough-sounding "laser-like" focus on instruction.

Furthermore, many policymakers and upper-level administrators seemed to miss out on an irony entailed in many of the reforms promoting teacher inquiry. If these reforms were to engender a genuine empowerment of teachers and a shift to a more transformational paradigm with distributed leadership, then upper-level administrators would need to modify their more traditional and transactional approaches (Friedman, 2004). Yet, high-stakes-testing environments hardly encouraged principals to take short-term risks that might yield long-term gains (Hargreaves & Shirley, 2009a). When they failed to do so, teachers responded with a sense of betrayal, once again exacerbating the mutually reinforcing microcultures of conservativism, individualism, and presentism.

Thus far in this account it might seem that teachers are the innocent victims of Machiavellian policymakers, Draconian administrators, and Voldemortian test designers. In point of fact, we do indeed believe that far too many pressures have been placed upon classroom teachers, and that the unrealistically high burdens are a major source of teacher attrition in our schools. Yet, simply blaming others is too easy. Educators are very much public servants; we are "street-level democrats" (Shirley, 2006a). Teachers themselves, through the advocacy of the American Federation of Teachers, played a major role in promoting and advancing standards-based reforms (Ravitch, 2000). Educators need to understand the sometimes desperate sense of public urgency about school improvement. Knee-jerk rebellion, in the form of those teachers who cross their arms and say "make me!" when learning about new practices that could benefit their pupils, can be just as mindless as unreflective compliance.

Teachers need space and time in which they can share instructional problems; modify curricula; and use data to improve pupil achievement. Teachers need settings in which they can think together and develop increasingly sophisticated levels of awareness about the full range of instructional options that they possess, especially when trying to engage students in learning who (for whatever reasons) have given up on themselves or who have developed anti-school ideologies of their own. Teachers possess disparate philosophies of education, and without opportunities for debating and clarifying the strengths and potential limitations of each perspective, their deeply held differences can lead to corrosive adversarial relationships that undermine community and relational trust (Achinstein, 2002). With such settings, on the other hand, teachers can attack the root problems causing alienated teaching and pupil resistance to schools, and by continually reflecting upon and modifying their work, they can improve it, not only reaching their pupils more effectively but also drawing more satisfaction and fulfillment from their vocations (Palmer, 1998).

This book provides one such setting. It is the product of many years of collaboration between a classroom teacher and a university professor. In composing the book, we have worked hard to combine a sense of the on-the-ground reality and expertise of an urban teacher with the research knowledge of a higher education colleague.

Although the entire book is the manifestation of this collaboration, at times the teacher's voice will dominate. At other times we will adapt a more academic tone. The book expresses our desire to bring more intellectual inquiry into teachers' cultures, while at the same time cultivating theory to give it more of a practical and applied dimension.

This introduction has been relatively abstract, but teachers do not experience alienated teaching as a disembodied idea. On the contrary, alienated teaching manifests itself as an intense lived experience. To illustrate this phenomenon, Chapter 1 provides a case study of an urban teacher in the midst of change. Chapter 2, entitled "Growing into Mindful Teaching," describes the origins of our Mindful Teacher seminar and its theoretical location at the nexus of research on teacher inquiry, Ellen Langer's cognitive approach to mindfulness, and diverse spiritual teachings. In Chapter 3 we describe the Mindful Teacher seminars. We delineate the eightfold structure we used to explore topics and the 10 clusters of questions teachers generated in the seminar setting. We provide anchoring illustrations of teachers who have engaged in mindful reflection on their work. These convey in concrete and practical ways the many challenges teachers have to work with today, as well as the resolutions that they found to meet specific difficulties.

Chapter 4 then develops a theoretical superstructure built off of the dynamics that emerged in the Mindful Teacher seminar setting.

We identify and describe seven synergies of mindful teaching—interrelated values and strategies that classroom teachers can use on a daily basis to integrate more reflection and attunement into their busy work lives. Because no set of formulas can ever resolve all of the complexities that emerge in a given classroom, we then articulate what we call the triple tensions of mindful teaching—contradictions that are embedded in the teaching relationship itself and that only briefly can be overcome as part of a dynamic process that unfolds over time.

In Chapter 5 we turn to the theme of mindful teacher leadership. If teachers are to overcome alienated teaching, this most likely will not unfold as a solitary act, but rather as a result of a series of nested activities that will require leadership from teachers themselves (Conway & Andrews, 2015). Mindful teacher leadership requires careful calibration because the lure of leadership, if not modulated and checked, can lead teachers away from rather than into the heart of teaching and learning (Cooper et al., 2015; Ogilby, 2007). To avoid such goal displacement, we conceptualize three domains of micro-, meso-, and macro-level change. We invite teachers to raise their professional expertise as they remain committed to and engaged with the students they teach on a daily basis.

Chapter 6 discusses the challenges presented to educators who wish to teach mindfully in an era of new digital technologies. For some, new technologies are a godsend, opening up the world for their students. For others, such technology can be a nightmare that perpetually distracts their students from real, in-depth learning. We chart a middle way between these two positions by using the seven synergies as a compass.

In the final, seventh chapter we move beyond the reflections and actions of individual educators to explore the diverse modalities of whole-school change through the lens of mindful teaching. What can school principals do to promote mindful teaching among their educators? Here we explore how mindful teaching can work its way up from individual classrooms so that it is developed coherently in schools and systems.

Mindfulness is a philosophical concept that many associate with Buddhism and meditation. We value those perspectives and their affiliated practices, but we primarily were attracted to the idea of mindful teaching as a response to real-life experiences that called out for resolution. We ask you to join us now as we describe those experiences from the vantage point of a midcareer urban public school teacher.

CHAPTER 1

The Great Divide

Liz MacDonald: Autobiographical Reflections

Like many individuals who find their way to teaching, I never planned on becoming an elementary school teacher as an undergraduate majoring in political science. However, when I moved home in the fall of 1995, I found myself in need of a job. Therefore I decided to sub in the Boston Public Schools (BPS). By late fall my subbing at different schools evolved into a long-term substitute position in a 1st-grade inclusion classroom. I didn't know the first thing about teaching, but things seemed to fall into place based on some natural intuition, endless hours of reading through teacher manuals, and the support of outstanding teacher colleagues.

Charlotte Haley and Ellen Murphy, different in their approaches but both exceptional and creative 1st-grade teachers, took me by the hand and walked me through the 1st grade. At the time, I didn't care whether they were whole-language or phonics people, black or white, teaching explicitly or implicitly, or constructivists or into direct instruction. I just needed ways to teach children! Both women modeled dedication to children and their cultures, and were incredibly supportive of me when the urban teaching experience would begin to overwhelm me. In retrospect, I'm pretty sure that I might well have left teaching were it not for their affirmations of my potential, their advice on complicated matters regarding communications with parents, and their unyielding belief in the potential of their students. They continually inspired me, and I thank them from the bottom of my heart.

What originally was simply a stopgap measure to buy time to think about my next career steps quickly became an all-consuming passion. Being in the presence of small children day after day brought me an endless supply of laughter and joy. At the same time, I was exasperated to discover that even though district mandates required the school to have a full-time aide in my inclusion classroom, no such aide was forthcoming in the cash-strapped district. This was the case even though I had one student with severe infant fetal alcohol syndrome who regularly wandered out of my class and generally operated with the cognitive abilities of a 3-year old. I discovered that one mother of a child in my class was being beaten by her husband, a professional who worked at a local university; I then helped the mother and her child to enter a women's shelter. I wondered why one boy was a perpetual torment to other children in class, but upon driving him to his after-school "program," I was stunned to drop him off in a crowded tenement with roughly 15 children in it and one health-care "provider" who spoke only Spanish (whereas the boy spoke only English).

Highly motivated to continue and improve my teaching, I subsequently entered a master's program and became certified in elementary education. I was completely immersed in teaching at this point. I would meet with BPS literacy coaches at coffee shops on weekends. I spent hours shopping for materials in teacher resource stores, and I attended as many workshops as I could that were offered by the BPS.

I had learned and was practicing every new teaching strategy I could get my hands on, and I felt that things looked the way that they should in my classroom. Still, I wasn't confident that my students were learning at an appropriate rate. Nonetheless, I did feel validated in 1999, when I was honored as one of five BPS teachers who received a Resident Teacher Award for exemplary practices.

Outside of my BPS world, I began engaging with grassroots organizations in Boston and developed professional development workshops on literacy in collaboration with the Massachusetts Department of Education that exposed me to a wide range of educators and policymakers. I continued to attend conferences and to collaborate with all kinds of instructors and specialists, and especially with colleagues at the Lynch School of Education at Boston College. I found myself evolving into a teacher leader.

By the spring of 2006 I became increasingly aware of contradictions in my life as an educator. Since 1999 I had mentored student teachers from Boston College in my classroom, and since 2001 I had taught sections of undergraduate and graduate teacher preparatory classes there. As a lecturer at Boston College, I encouraged teacher candidates to explore a full range of diverse instructional practices in their teaching. Ironically, however, in my own 4th-grade classroom I found that my teaching was not promoting the learning gains for which I had hoped. As a teacher at the higher education level, I felt idealistic, and I could tell that many student teachers looked up to me, but in my own classroom I questioned my abilities and was painfully aware of the slow progress some of my students were making. To a certain extent, I felt more anguish than I had felt in my first year of teaching because now I knew so much more, but I was still unable to translate that knowledge into pupil learning gains. All too often I found myself at my wits' end, especially when working with several pupils who were learning, but at a slower pace than the policymakers who created the Massachusetts Comprehensive Assessment System (MCAS) test would have found acceptable.

My experience of the disconnection between my efficacy in the higher education classroom and my struggles in my elementary school led to me to a series of extended dialogues with colleagues at both the university and primary levels. Why was it that I felt I could teach others how to teach, but was so challenged in my own classroom? Upon further investigation, I came to discover that on several occasions I was engaging in classroom practices not because I thought that they were best for my pupils, but rather because I thought that they were what I was supposed to do. I was acquiescing in teaching practices that felt artificial to me, and I did so primarily out of a sense of deference to the district. Upon reflection, I observed that pupil misbehavior was greatest when I was using practices that I believed in the least.

What kinds of examples of district-mandated practices had I adopted? Ironically, most of them were drawn from the repertoire of child-centered, inquiry-driven practices that I believed in and that I promoted in my teacher education classes. The BPS mandated the use of Readers and Writers Workshop (www.readersandwritersworkshop.com) and TERC mathematics (www2.terc.edu/), both constructivist approaches to curriculum and instruction. The district required elementary school teachers to provide instruction and affiliated activities for 2 hours a day in the language arts and 70 minutes a day in mathematics. Significantly, it was not so much the actual content of these practices as it was the nature of their implementation that appeared to create difficulties.

My experiences in this regard are supported by scholars who have researched the impact of mandated changes on teachers (Bailey, 2000; Cohen, 1990; Hargreaves, 2004). According to this research, one of the major problems of educational change occurs when teachers are asked to shift from one instructional approach to another with inadequate support. When I first began teaching in Boston, my school used a Houghton-Mifflin basal reading anthology and the John Collins Writing Folder program. The latter dictated what genres the students should be writing in, along with what specific writing skills should be taught. I didn't like this highly structured program because my students rarely had the opportunity to write about subjects that interested them.

Under the leadership of Superintendent Thomas Payzant, the BPS subsequently abolished both the basal readers and the writing folders and implemented the Readers and Writers Workshop. Embedded in the Workshop's philosophy is the tenet that students need to have choices over what they write and that their writing should be modeled after published writers' work using "mentor texts." I was among the first cohort of teachers in the district to receive professional development in the Workshop model. Even though I had many questions about the model, I began implementation in my 4th-grade classroom before the mandate was implemented in my school.

I was pleased to discover that my own pedagogy of teaching writing mirrored much of what I understood Writers Workshop to advocate. I believed that students needed choices, that they could learn through examples of good writing, and that their writing should be taken from one stage to the next through individual conferencing. However, the lack of accompanying materials, other than mentor texts, and the absence of a curriculum guide left me somewhat uncertain as to what to teach and when.

Following the structure of the Workshop model, I taught 15-minute mini-lessons, allowed the students to write in their notebooks for 35 minutes, and subsequently had the whole class discuss their writing for the last 10 minutes. Having no specified curriculum other than the state standards, I struggled to plan mini-lessons each day. Because a majority of my students performed below grade level and many were English language learners, writing for 35 minutes without interruption was a major challenge for them. Some students began doodling, others distracted one another by poking or prodding their neighbors, and some simply wrote lyrics from rap songs over and over again. I found that conferencing regularly with each student—as is called for by the Writers Workshop—was an enormous challenge because so many students were easily distracted when I was focused on a single student.

I experienced similar difficulties with math reforms. In an attempt to implement TERC mathematics systematically districtwide, the school system's math department created a pacing guide outlining which investigations (lessons) should be taught each day at each grade level throughout the district. A district mandate sought to ensure consistency and continuity in math instruction across schools. TERC is a spiral curriculum, weaving mathematical concepts in each unit of study throughout the year and building upon concepts and strategies introduced at previous grade levels. Theoretically, full implementation of the program is essential to its success.

Like many of my colleagues, I found that it was a challenge to keep up with the pacing guide's schedule. Other teachers in the district, like me, encountered students every day whose conceptual understanding and basic mathematical skills were so limited that more time needed to be spent with a single investigation. For example, an investigation might require pupils to solve a complex multiplication word story. When my students tried to solve such problems, I often discovered that they not only lacked proficiency in multiplication facts, but had a weak understanding of the concept of multiplication itself. At these junctures I knew that my pupils needed additional time to learn about multiplication, but the pacing guide made it difficult to take the time to remediate my struggling learners. In such instances, I usually chose to follow the pacing guide rather than dig down deeper into content, in part because my pupils were tested every 4 to 6 weeks. I believe that the times when I made that decision to follow the pacing guide coincided with a rise in students' behavioral difficulties, and their learning was at its lowest level.

Research shows that the best-intentioned and most-research-grounded reforms often break down at the level of implementation (Cohen, 1990; McLaughlin, 2006; Pressman & Wildavsky, 1973). When I presented these obstacles of teaching and learning to coaches in my district, I felt that I did not receive assistance but simply was met with the assertion that I needed to find a way to make the Workshop model successful. I felt that I was at fault. It was as if there were no flaws in the Workshop itself, but only in my delivery of instruction and my organization of the classroom. This sense of failure was especially exasperating to me because I had welcomed the Readers and Writers Workshop as a creative alternative to the John Collins Writing Folder. Frustrated by the lack of support and questioning my abilities as a teacher, I continued using the Readers and Writers Workshop despite my intuition that I was not providing optimal instruction for my students.

Like many teachers, I really made a good-faith effort to implement my school district's curriculum and to comply with mandated reforms. I always was on the lookout for new resources to incorporate into my lessons throughout the year. Some of those resources took me far away from the Readers and Writers Workshop approach. For example, I found that some familiarity with systematic phonics provided me with a broader repertoire of teaching practices that benefited some of my struggling readers and writers. I learned that there were many sides to the literacy wars, that it went against my nature to choose one side and enter into battle with the other, and that I wanted to remain open to and inclusive of the full array of instructional approaches that different reformers advocated.

What kinds of instructional practices did I want to use? In addition to my role as a facilitator of pupils' knowledge construction, as advocated by Readers and Writers Workshop and TERC, I wanted to take advantage of a wide range of practices that would allow me to share my own zest for continual learning and my enthusiasm for literature and mathematics with my pupils. I felt that I needed more structure in terms of using the Readers and Writers Workshop and wanted to know that I was covering all of the reading skills that my students needed. I wanted children to learn several ways of conceptualizing mathematics problems, but I also wanted to make sure that they were comfortable with a certain amount of memorization in mathematics so that they were prepared for state tests when they needed to recall information about multiplication tables at a moment's notice. Although I liked the emphasis on children thinking for themselves and in small groups, I believed that these activities needed to be supplemented with well-designed teacher-led instruction to make sure that the children had new knowledge on which to scaffold their extended learning activities.

These critical reflections then led me to question many of aspects of the culture of urban educational reform today. Can teaching ever be excellent when teachers use practices that we believe are of limited value to children? What kinds of cultural spaces are available to teachers to share our misgivings about instructional programs, or to adapt them selectively into our preexisting repertoire of practices? Are students able to detect when teachers are using practices that we ourselves are skeptical about?

CONCEPTUALIZING ALIENATED TEACHING

Derived from the sociological theory of alienated labor (Marx, 1982), alienated teaching describes instructional processes in which teachers neglect teaching practices that they believe are best suited for their pupils and instead comply with externally imposed mandates out of a sense of deference to authority. Research indicates that teachers' compliance comes at a considerable cost, as teachers' loss of professional autonomy and agency can lead to low morale, a loss of self-efficacy, and disinvestment from teaching (Bailey, 2000; Craig, 2006; Hargreaves & Fink, 2006). Alienated teaching is especially problematic because of the emotionally charged nature of teaching and learning (Fried, 1995; Hargreaves, 1994; Nieto, 2003; Stone-Johnson, 2015).

Teachers can take multiple routes in responding to the dilemmas just described. For example, there is the strategy of protest. In this scenario, they dissent from the district's mandates and argue against the erosion of teacher autonomy. Such protest comes at a high cost to teachers, for although they may not actually be fired for failing to comply, they can suffer loss of professional status as a result of public disagreement with reforms. Dissident teachers can be punished by having their teaching positions or their grade levels reassigned from year to year.

A second strategy would be loyalty. Teachers acknowledge that they are not high up in the hierarchy of school systems; therefore, they accommodate new mandates the best they can. They cast off previous practices with regret but do not dwell on them, and they align their instruction to new standards. They "go along to get along," avoid catastrophizing about unfortunate aspects of reforms, and capitalize on positive aspects of reform to the best of their abilities.

In a third option, teachers go underground, shutting the door and carrying on surreptitious revolts as lone rebels. Part of this strategy can entail waiting until a new superintendent comes, anticipating that the pedagogical pendulum will swing back in a familiar direction with enough patience and luck. This option of privatized teaching is popular among many veteran teachers, who have tired of the perpetual merry-go-round of reform initiatives and prefer simply to hone their craft in the solitude of the cellular classroom.

Finally, a fourth option involves exit. Nationally, more than 41% of beginning teachers in urban school systems exercise this route in their first 5 years of teaching (Perda, 2013). The ability to exercise professional autonomy is among the most important criteria in teachers' job satisfaction (Ingersoll, 2003; Ingersoll, Merrill, & Stuckey, 2014). When beginning teachers experience that such autonomy is not to be a part of their professional identity, they reassess their career choices and often seek employment elsewhere (Torres, 2012). Teacher attrition has a detrimental impact on student achievement; research shows that students perform better on tests when they are taught by those with additional experience beyond the first few years (Henry,

Fortner, & Bastian, 2012). Teacher turnover has been estimated to cost the United States over $2.2 billion annually (Alliance for Excellent Education, 2014). It reflects a profound failure to support the nation's educators adequately.

Liz MacDonald: Continued Reflections

In my case, my response to these dilemmas was complicated. As a general principle, I endorsed the open-ended approaches of Readers and Writers Workshop and constructivist mathematics mandated by the BPS. I felt fortunate to work in a district where the cultivation of children's abilities as independent thinkers and problem solvers was at the center of school improvement efforts. Furthermore, I had begun an exciting collaboration with Professor Maria Estela Brisk of Boston College on teaching English language learners, resulting in my first academic publication (Brisk et al., 2002). I was not interested in demonizing the school system, which I believed was led by many conscientious individuals who genuinely had the children's best interests at heart. Hence, the stance of protest did not seem to me especially valuable, because I found much that was praiseworthy in the reforms that privileged Readers and Writers Workshop and TERC investigations. Rather, it was their externally mandated nature and lack of high-quality, ongoing support that was problematic. I had no desire to exit urban schools or teaching altogether. I did not wish to conceal my teaching practices by shutting my classroom doors, and I wanted to be as public and open in my philosophy and practices of education as possible.

In the summer of 2005 I conducted professional development workshops for urban teachers as part of a consultancy with the Massachusetts Department of Education. While working with other classroom teachers, I learned that many other educators shared my experience of alienated teaching. Teachers would ask me questions about how much freedom they had to stray from the selected reading program in order to modify and supplement the curriculum to meet the needs of their students, worrying that they might go too far and get in trouble with their principals or superintendents. Many teachers appeared fearful of district reprisals if they departed from prescribed pedagogical strategies or curricula, even if the supplementary materials had many intrinsic merits and might especially appeal to diverse pupils in urban environments. Some teachers reported that school officials locked away their old curricula when new ones arrived so that teachers would only be allowed to use the new program's materials. At one low-performing school in the state, a teacher informed me that she stopped a common reading practice in her classroom because a publishing company representative told her it did not fit into the company's program. When I asked the teacher whether she thought that previous practice was beneficial, she replied that it had indeed benefited her pupils—and that she didn't know why she had given it up. These conversations led me to recognize how fragile teacher professionalism is today, and how needful teachers are of continual support and guidance from their colleagues, administrators, and the public in general.

To deal with these challenges, I sought ideas, dialogues, and resources that could help me with the dilemma of alienated teaching. I wanted to avoid a polarizing, simplistic debate that would pit me as a classroom teacher against my urban public school system. I knew that the BPS budgets were stretched thin, that BPS policies often reflected rather than manufactured larger social inequalities, and that our schools were in need of teacher leadership in buildings throughout the district.

Yet where could I turn for support?

By the spring of 2005 I was at a breaking point in my instruction. Even though I had taught for 10 years in the BPS, had won professional accolades, and was a widely recognized teacher leader, in my own 4th-grade classroom I was all too aware of my frailties and shortcomings. I found myself preoccupied by one boy with a severe case of attention deficit hyperactivity disorder (ADHD) who could turn the best-planned lesson into chaos for the whole class, by a girl who was struggling with her math and cried daily because she was fearful of not being promoted along with her cohort, and by several students who I knew were highly capable but simply did not appear motivated enough to devote themselves to their academic achievement. I was exerting a tremendous amount of energy in my teaching and spending hours outside of the school day in planning how to make things right. I felt like I was running up Heartbreak Hill and the peak was nowhere in sight.

THE IMPORTANCE OF LEADERSHIP

How can one recognize when one is falling into patterns of alienated teaching and imbuing remote policymakers with more control of one's daily interactions with children than they deserve? Resignation and demoralization don't often happen all at once but rather in slow increments over time. Teachers experience a loss of morale as an individual psychological symptom, failing to see that their difficulties are social in origin. How can one keep good teachers in the classroom, not out of self-abnegation, but out of genuine love of children and fulfillment in meeting real educational needs?

As indicated earlier, we have no silver bullets to shoot into the educational policy arena. Being a good teacher is extraordinarily demanding work. If one really cares about teaching, one is perpetually reinventing lessons, hunting out new materials to engage disaffected pupils, and learning from colleagues and from research about new ways to modify curricula and group activities. All of this tinkering is the heart and soul of teachers' daily practice, and making sure that good teachers possess the tools and cultural settings in which they can flourish is the responsibility of educational leaders, policymakers, and the public at large.

Good teaching will always be hard, and it will always be harder in environments that are underresourced and that suffer from long-standing social inequities. There will always be complicated pupils, intrusive parents, and controlling administrators. The more that one promotes simplified agendas to solve all of these prosaic problems of everyday life, the more that one raises false expectations and contributes to the air of unreality and fads that shape far too many educational contexts.

As one settles into teaching as a career and begins to realize that an educational utopia really isn't right around the corner, one realizes that one is going to need to build regular networks of support into one's work routines. In our case, we first began collaborating on a Title II Teacher Quality Enhancement (TQE) grant funded by the U.S. Department of Education that promoted school and university collaborations. The TQE grants provided funding to restructure colleges and university-based teacher education programs to encourage experimental partnerships to support urban schools.

Our particular grant linked seven colleges and universities—Boston College, the University of Massachusetts at Amherst, the University of Massachusetts at Boston, Clark University, Lesley University, Northeastern University, and Wheelock College—with 18 urban schools in Boston, Springfield, and Worcester. The grant provided our Massachusetts Coalition for Teacher Quality and Student Achievement with $7.2 million of funding spread over 6 years.

With support from the grant, we began team-teaching across our school and university boundaries to learn more about each other's challenges and to embed teacher preparatory activities in real urban school environments (Shirley, 2006a, 2006b; Shirley et al., 2006). We came to know each other and many of each other's colleagues through the federal funding, which provided us with resources to host summer conferences for extended learning about challenges and opportunities in urban schools and communities. Along with our other school and university colleagues, we attended conferences and presented our work at the annual meetings of the American Educational Research Association and the American Association of Colleges of Teacher Education. These joint activities, shared with many others and integrated into our teacher education practices, allowed us to build trust and confidence in one another. They taught us that concrete steps could be taken as individuals and collectively not only to overcome the great divide, but also to create a new and dynamic collaboration with a life of its own.

Although funding from Title II on the one hand represented an unprecedented opportunity to support school and university partnerships, it also raised sensitive turf issues of control and power both within and across institutional settings. Why is it that so few teacher education courses in higher education institutions are offered in collaboration with experienced urban teachers? Why is it that colleges and universities can skim off huge amounts of money in overhead expenses related to running grant-funded projects? What happens when budget cutbacks in a system like the BPS threaten to destroy carefully nourished partnership activities, and higher education institutions are left absorbing what were originally planned to be shared expenditures? And how can the fragile human relationships that are built across institutional lines by boundary spanners be preserved when some upper-level administrators, unfamiliar with the need to adapt their leadership styles, unintentionally undermine partnerships by following protocols rigidly rather than adjusting rules to serve the larger public good?

When we first began team-teaching, we realized that weekly meetings were going to be imperative. After a couple of early forays panned out, we settled on Jim's Deli, a bustling restaurant a couple of miles away from Garfield Elementary School. It was at Jim's where we developed the idea of a mindful teacher project, which is described more fully in the next chapter.

CHAPTER 2

Growing into Mindful Teaching

One might ask at this juncture something along the following lines: "What's the big deal? New policies are always coming along. Educators are professionals, so one should always use one's professional discretion; it's one's right. Take what you want from the Readers and Writers Workshop and TERC investigations, and ignore the rest. Don't get bogged down in literal interpretations of new mandates."

How easy it sounds! This (only apparently wise) advice ignores the high-pressure educational policy context of recent years. David Hopkins, a leading school improvement thinker in the United Kingdom, has described the "policy epidemic" that is sweeping developed nations, in which legislators have placed enormous expectations upon school systems to rectify longstanding social injustices that exceed their capacity to improve (2001, p. 4). This "pathology of central policy change" (Hopkins, 2001 p. 4) created anxiety and guilt for conscientious educators for years, who have burned the midnight oil trying to find research that will help them to pump up their test scores an extra notch in search of adequate yearly progress.

Yet just when one might seek to stigmatize policymakers as witless Gradgrinds of educational change, we would rather argue the opposite: that one must give credit for the innovative and emancipatory dimensions of some policy reforms. The Title II grants that funded the Massachusetts Coalition, for example, gave us valuable resources from which we could learn about the modalities of educational change in the three largest urban school districts in Massachusetts, could organize workshops and annual summer institutes with student and teacher participation from urban high schools, and could encourage reticent faculty in both the urban public schools and the higher education institutions to venture into one another's classrooms to develop a variety of innovative and engaging learning activities.

These diverse experiences with colleagues from around the state were enormously broadening and helped us to traverse the limitations of our respective school and higher education settings. In a very real way, an entity like the Massachusetts Coalition represented an enactment of John Dewey's philosophy of democratic education, which hinged upon drawing together diverse constituencies and enabling them to identify common interests to promote the public good (Dewey, 1916). Although we had not yet come up with the term *alienated teaching* at the time, we knew that something was wrong with most mainstream reform movements and that we wanted to find a way of addressing it. Unfortunately, most grant-funded activities require applicants to endorse the funders' assumptions as the point of departure and provide little flexibility for a classroom teacher and professor to develop their own agenda.

Our own situation provided a happy exception in this regard. For years the BPS and Boston College had collaborated in mutual activities, and this collegiality had become institutionalized in the form of Boston Collaborative Fellows grants that were administered by Boston College and BPS, collectively. We applied for and received a grant to launch a "mindful teacher" project that would provide us with stipends for cohorts of BPS teachers who would be willing to join us in a seminar structure entailing common readings, reflection on teaching practices, journal entries, classroom visits, an online chat room, and a research project. The seminars would be designed to provide participants with opportunities to reflect upon their teaching, to discuss ongoing curricular reforms in the BPS, and to learn about new teaching strategies, and to do so in a collegial setting. Above all, we wanted to get past the perpetual merry-go-round of fads and innovations to explore a deeper side of education, should it be accessible to us.

Yet identifying many of the problems of educational change hardly is the same thing as coming up with sensible alternatives. To begin to move in this direction, we consulted three separate streams of thought.

PROFESSIONAL LEARNING COMMUNITIES

First, we explored the large body of research on teacher inquiry as enacted in what scholars describe as "professional learning communities" (Stoll & Louis, 2007). Recall that many years ago Dan Lortie described teachers' microcultures as trapped in a vicious circle of individualism, conservatism, and presentism (Lortie, 1975). Although there is variation in the outcomes data, it appears that when successfully organized and led, professional learning communities provide valuable levers for teachers by enhancing their human, social, and decisional capital (Hargreaves & Fullan, 2012). They help teachers to break out of their isolation and to provide professional support for one another. One can tell when a professional learning community has achieved take-off when one finds previously isolated teachers sharing lesson plans and information about their pupils (Wells & Feun, 2013). As they do so, teachers develop new forms of distributed leadership that make the decisive difference between a "learning-enriched" and a "learning-impoverished" environment (Rosenholtz, 1989).

Reviewing the literature on professional learning communities, we found a number of similarities among scholars and practitioners, with a variety of different emphases in terms of research methodologies and policy recommendations. In one of the most well-known variants, Donald Schön (1987) popularized the notion of the "reflective practitioner" who goes beyond a direct assimilation of information to conceptualize one's work in a creative manner that can circumvent established protocols to develop more powerful and efficacious ways of meeting one's goals. Patricia King and Karen Strohm Kitchener (1994) developed a model of reflective judgment that had more empirical foundations than Schön's work and encouraged the development of critical thinking and informed professional autonomy. These works have important European analogues in what some have described as the German tradition of didactic analysis that has been a foundational part of teacher education in Europe for decades (Shirley, 2008a, 2008b; Westbury, Hopmann, & Riquarts, 2000).

Much of the literature on teacher inquiry and teacher leadership incorporates notions of collaborative reflection, discussion, evaluation, and action (Blankstein, Houston, & Cole, 2008). A number of these concepts and practices have important affinities with Paolo Freire's (2000, p. 97) concept of the "generative theme" that is elaborated by teacher researchers within a "cultural circle" of adult learners. Although there have been debates for many years about the significance of teacher inquiry and reflective practice (Liston & Zeichner, 1990; Selman, 1988), the debates share a number of assumptions. For example, the authors all value the here-and-now quality of classroom interaction. The researchers all emphasize the need for teachers to question their assumptions about teaching and learning in the light of new findings about their pupils. Likewise, they all view teaching as a genuinely intellectual activity in which even the smallest choices contain ethical and political dimensions that call forth the highest kinds of reflection and judgment.

Sonia Nieto, for example, has a section in her enormously popular and teacher-friendly book *What Keeps Teachers Going?* entitled "Obsessed by Mindful Teaching" (Nieto, 2003, pp. 88–89). In that section she describes Stephen Gordon, an accomplished BPS teacher who expressed an anguished confusion about the best way to reach his urban pupils. In Nieto's account, accepting the raw emotional vulnerability of teaching, and learning to share that with others, can help one to penetrate to the core meaning of teaching as a vocation. In this interpretation, mindfulness requires a full engagement with the existential complexity of teaching in all of its emotional, interpersonal, and even spiritual plenitude.

As professional learning communities (PLCs) have proliferated, researchers (Hargreaves & Fink, 2006; Hargreaves & Shirley, 2009a) have raised concerns that in some cases they have become subtly coercive, so that rather than providing teachers with genuine opportunities for probing deeply into issues of teaching and learning, they have instead become thinly veiled venues for staging "contrived collegiality" (Hargreaves, 1994, p. 186). Others (Murrell, 2001; Noguera, 2008; Payne, 2008) have cautioned that PLCs in too many cases have become narrowly technical in their orientations and have marginalized important discussions of race, ethnicity, and power from their deliberations. With much of the recent drive for raising academic achievement, it appears that PLCs in too many settings developed an exclusive focus on data-driven decision making, such that any other ways of conceptualizing teachers' reflective inquiry were marginalized and discredited. In these instances, teachers have become "data-driven to distraction" (Shirley & Hargreaves, 2006). Although we cannot comment on how widespread such distortions have become, we do know that in the mindful teacher project we wanted to avoid such constraints.

ELLEN LANGER'S STUDIES OF MINDFULNESS

Second, we were drawn to the research of psychologist Ellen Langer (1989, 1997), who has long been interested in habits of mind that lead individuals to overlook potential solutions to everyday problems. For Langer, mindfulness entails "openness to novelty," "alertness to distinction," "sensitivity to different contexts," "awareness of multiple perspectives," and "orientation in the present" (1997, p. 23). A mindful individual, in this understanding, never looks at a sunrise and views it as the same thing day after day, but instead attends to aspects of light, color, and inner experience that make it an entirely unprecedented event. A mindful teacher, by implication, could never look at a student and reduce him or her to a single attribute, but always would be on the lookout for new ways in which the student could be learning or developing.

Langer's studies show that mindfulness can be learned. Although we all are creatures of habit, we are skilled at overcoming past habits when we discover new and better ways of solving hitherto intractable problems. But we need activity settings to go beyond top-down instruction on the one hand and disconnected bottom-up initiatives on the other. With the right kinds of settings—such as well-designed professional learning communities for teachers—we can be "jostled into mindful awareness" (1997, p. 24). We can learn to solve complex problems by looking at them in new ways with supportive and nonjudgmental colleagues.

Langer's approach was appealing to us because of its empiricism and her witty, zestful writing style. In her insistence that there are many ways to conceptualize problems and her interest in exploring unorthodox strategies for solving practical issues of everyday life, Langer opened up new venues for teachers to think beyond the constraints of their busy work lives and to come up with their own independent strategies for improving their students' learning.

SPIRITUALITY

Separate from these recent developments in the social sciences—and most challenging for our future investigations—mindfulness is a central concept in the world's diverse religious and philosophical traditions.

Classic Buddhist sutras, such as the Heart Sutra and the Diamond Sutra, articulate notions of mindfulness that encourage sensitivity to the here-and-now sensations of the moment, compassion for all living beings, and ethical maxims for proper conduct (Hanh, 1988, 1992). Martin Buber's *I and Thou* advocates the importance of moving beyond an instrumental, *I-it* orientation to others to attain a more sacred and mindful *I-thou* sensitivity to others as ends in themselves, with reference to the Kabbalic mysticism of Judaism. Mindful discernment is a key component of the pedagogy of Saint Ignatius of Loyola, the founder of the Society of Jesus in the Catholic Church. In each case, diverse thinkers have endeavored to find ways to harmonize the care of the self with one's responsibilities to others and to the natural world. Attending to inner growth is not viewed as narcissistic self-indulgence, but as a profound ethical responsibility. Neglecting the care of one's inner spiritual life, it is believed, will inevitably have negative consequences not just for the individual, but for others as well.

Scholars (e.g., Miller, 2015) recently have documented that children and adolescents with strong spiritual beliefs demonstrate greater resilience in the face of adversity. These beliefs provide both the young and adults with valuable resources for thinking through life's challenges and for creating real and lasting solutions. The First Amendment of the Bill of Rights in the U.S. Constitution guarantees the separation of church and state, but this need not be so construed that spirituality must be left out of public education. It simply needs to be understood and utilized in a generous and inclusive way.

When we first began the Mindful Teacher seminars, we drew extensively upon the "Engaged Buddhism" of Thich Nhat Hanh. We read from the writings of this gentle Zen master, including his 14 mindfulness trainings, and practiced meditation together. The first of the mindfulness trainings, advocating "detachment from views," was especially important in establishing an atmosphere of openness to diverse perspectives during our meetings.

As the seminars progressed, however, it became evident that too much of an explicit reference to Buddhism was experienced as exclusionary by some of the teachers who valued prayer as a personal expression of their religious beliefs. We decided then to adjust the culture of our seminars. We retained meditation in the form of a simple calming exercise to quiet the body and focus the mind. We wanted the seminars to support all of our participants, including those atheists and agnostics whose spirituality is too often unrecognized or discounted.

The purpose of the seminars was to support teachers in challenging circumstances, not to develop them as disciples of any particular belief system or philosophy.

AN INTEGRATIVE APPROACH

These three strands—teacher inquiry in professional learning communities, Langer's mindfulness research, and spirituality—provided the conceptual underpinnings that we brought to our Mindful Teacher seminars. Yet our enactment of ideas from these three strands is very much our own ensemble of activities and values. Without disrespecting the enormous intellectual and spiritual contributions made from each of the three strands, our goal was not so much to master their respective bodies of knowledge as it was to appropriate them, with a light touch, to enable us to better understand our interactions with our students and colleagues in our own classrooms and schools. Because schools are incredibly rich cultural settings, even the briefest of excursions into of individual classrooms provides abundant material for reflection and action.

Our goal in the seminars was to take some tentative first steps and to explore the concept of mindfulness in our professional lives. Some of our participants preferred Langer's definition of mindfulness as cognition, without any necessary accompaniment of formal meditation practice. Others very much valued meditation as a way to calm their bodies, focus their minds, and then think more clearly about potential solutions to their challenges. While we discussed these shifting understandings of mindfulness in the seminars, it was not our role as seminar leaders to pass judgment on participants' preferences. To do so would have betrayed the very purpose of the seminars and imposed classificatory schemes on participants that could have hindered their future growth (Maslow, 1969).

This, then, is the kernel of our understanding of mindful teaching in the contemporary educational context. It entails recognizing that beyond the push for standards, accountability, alignment, and data-driven decision making, an alternate reality has emerged, full of contradictions, messiness, and "human, all-too-human" problems. Yet with this acknowledgment comes splendid opportunities to advance real learning—not just test prep, or gaming the system, or the kind of reform that cuts out recess in the name of academic rigor.

Education can only improve when teachers themselves have opportunities to become more reflective concerning the multiple pressures upon them and collaborate to build professional learning communities that promote deep and sustained thinking and analysis about the many problems in schools, and especially those in urban settings. Reformers often want all teachers to "be on the same page" and to "get everyone on board," but the reality is that educators often have different, and sometimes opposing, philosophies of education that originate in their different life experiences. A good educational system draws upon these diverse experiences to create cultures that harmonize their disparate aspects in the interest of improving the human condition for generations to come.

Educators need activity settings to explore those differences and to discern both their benefits as well as their potential costs. Rather than suppressing their differences, teachers need ways of bringing them to light, discussing their strengths and potential weaknesses, and making them pedagogically generative. This in turn requires that teachers work in schools in which they are able to develop their capacities to innovate so that established practices are compared continuously with new and different approaches to instruction and curriculum design (Emo, 2015). Ideally, teachers in the future will be able to work in schools that integrate their personal pedagogies and schoolwide pedagogies. Good schools enable their teachers to oscillate back and forth between individualistic tinkering and refining of lessons along with collective professionalism in the form of schoolwide pedagogies (Conway & Andrews, 2015).

THE PROFESSIONAL STAKES FOR TEACHERS

If mindful teaching occurs at the nexus of policy and instruction, then it must go beyond the simple adjustment of a teaching strategy here and a curriculum supplement there. At stake in these considerations is the very professional identity of teachers. We are working with an understanding of teaching that acknowledges and cherishes its tentative, experimental, iterative nature. We have tried enough different varieties of frontal instruction, small-group instruction, individualized curricula, and alternative forms of assessment to appreciate that every approach has strengths and weaknesses. We have observed enough teachers to have learned just how personalized and customized teaching needs to be, and how new practices cannot simply be plopped down onto preexisting routines without a process of complex mutual adjustment between a teacher and a new program over time. Our contention is that teachers' professionalism relies on our ability to see multiple sides of the decisions that we make and to make informed judgments about which tools to use to provide the best instruction possible.

Accepting this open-endedness of education allows us to view teachers' professional decision making not as a problem to be avoided through impulsive overreaction to test scores or uncritical compliance with mandates, but rather as *an intellectual field in and of itself*. What do teachers think of recent reforms? How do they cope on both emotional and professional levels with performance expectations? How can policies better respect teachers' lived experiences in the classroom and make the most of them to improve their students' learning? We seek to preserve and expand this fragile domain of teachers' professional learning and action that is so easily abrogated when political reformers of whatever stripe—be they liberal, conservative, or radical—move into the heart of teaching and learning.

Given the recent massive policy shifts in U.S. education, we have found it easy to strike up a conversation with virtually every urban public school teacher we have met, both in Boston and across the country, around the concept of alienated teaching. Teachers know all too well the loss of locus of control and boundary invasion that occurs when shifting policy agendas move into their instructional activities. It is important to note that many teachers do not have a language with which to describe alienated teaching. The dominant phrase is simply the laconic "burnout," which psychologizes what are in fact social processes. The magnitude of teacher attrition indicates that it is not a problem of individual teachers but of workplace conditions that lead to such frequent turnover amongst staff. Yet, what occurs when we share the concept of mindful teaching with educators and pilot contemplative practices intended to enhance mindfulness? How do teachers subsequently endeavor to adapt their instruction in their classroom and schools in light of literature and practices affiliated with mindfulness?

To answer these queries, we now turn to the Mindful Teacher seminars themselves.

CHAPTER 3

Practicing Mindfully

Thus far we have set up an opposition between *alienated* teaching, which is coercive, privatized, and resented, and *mindful* teaching, which is integrative, reflective, and deep. But it may not be so easy to move from one experience of teaching to the other, and our criticism of alienated teaching might be more easily stated than avoided. German philosopher of education Lothar Klingberg (1990) argued in his theory of dialectical didactics that there are always power asymmetries at work in education, and that students and teachers, even if they long for deeper relationships, often cannot resist tendencies to objectify and instrumentalize one another. The tradition of Socratic dialogues has long held that a moment of alienation in the form of cognitive dissonance is crucial to get learners out of their comfort zones and open to new ideas. And we know from many years of experiments in group work in social change organizations that even when individuals have the best of intentions, subtle differences in styles of communication—such as tone of voice, eye contact, and other forms of body language—have powerful influences in how groups evolve (Pallotta, 2004).

The Mindful Teacher seminars that we established had no magic potions to offer in regard to these dilemmas. Nor did we promise to concoct such potions. Rather, we wanted to *befriend* the complex and the intractable, anticipating that perhaps if we changed our frame of reference, we might come to understand our own teaching and learning differently and could convey that new understanding to children in rewarding ways.

To help you understand how we endeavored to do this, and with what consequences and outcomes, we shall now do the following:

- Describe the eightfold structure of the Mindful Teacher seminars;

- Identify 10 clusters of questions engendered through seminar discussions; and
- Provide six anchoring illustrations of how seminar participants demonstrated aspects of mindfulness to reconceptualize and improve their work as educators.

Liz MacDonald: The Knot of Needfulness

As a teacher in the school district, I knew that the Boston Public Schools offered high-quality professional development in innovative reading, writing, and mathematics teaching practices along with training for teachers in systematic intervention programs that were well recognized among special educators. More recently the district was offering professional development around the achievement gap and cultural competency. All of this professional development was relevant and beneficial. Still, what the district was not adequately offering teachers was a place where they could be emotionally, intellectually, and professionally supported in a collegial setting. There were not many settings provided— other than perhaps the local pub of a school's neighborhood—where teachers were able to discuss the emotional demands of urban teaching. And more often than not, these informal settings that teachers found outside of school to vent about the daily challenges of teaching tended to turn into complaining sessions rather than opportunities for real reflection or productive planning.

Working collaboratively with faculty at Boston College, I was able to experience the scholarly side of the education world. I was able to stay current with educational research, and I had the opportunity to attend national and international conferences. Yet I wasn't fully satisfied. I wanted my fellow teachers to be able to experience this world and have their sense of professionalism enhanced, even though I knew that there was still a slight disconnect between educational research and classroom practice and realized that reading research and attending conferences would not be enough. Believing that urban school teachers needed a place to discuss the emotional wear and tear of the classroom, I felt we needed a new kind of setting—a new "zone of mediation" in the words of one scholar (Welner, 2001, p. 94)—where teachers could share the many different questions that arose in the course of their everyday classroom realities.

CREATING THE MINDFUL TEACHER SEMINARS

It's one thing to attempt to create a setting in which teachers can develop and seek to answer their questions—and quite another to have success in doing so. The resolution to the questions generated by teachers, we believed, could only come through testing our ideas out in practice and by attempting to establish a tone of open and respectful inquiry that provided enough structure and coherence that teachers would be able to move quickly and productively into topics that concerned them. In our experience, a few preliminary ingredients were essential in getting things off to a good start. First, we had a highly recognized teacher leader who was more than willing to discuss challenges in her own classroom. Second, we had a university-based scholar who would prepare readings and lead discussions on what research had to say about teachers' different concerns. Third, we had a neutral setting on the Boston College campus that provided a splendid physical locale for meetings. Finally, we had stipends for teachers, provided through the Boston Collaborative Fellows grant, to match and even surpass district funds for professional development.

We developed a series of Saturday "Mindful Teacher" seminars, in which we met to discuss readings, to practice formal meditation, and to explore topics of relevance and concern for the teachers. Here we wanted to provide participants with material for intellectual development, and to do so in such a way that they could make connections to their everyday lives as classroom teachers. We read Ellen Langer's *The Power of Mindful Learning* (1997), Sonia Nieto's *What Keeps Teachers Going?* (2003), Thich Nhat Hanh's "Fourteen Mindfulness Trainings" (1998), and Ann Lieberman and Lynne Miller's *Teacher Leadership* (2004). In addition, we purchased Jon Kabat-Zinn's meditation CDs (www.mindfulnesstapes.com). We encouraged the teachers to meditate on their own as part of a regular formal mindfulness practice.

The organization of our Mindful Teacher seminars followed a common pattern. Participants would arrive at the Boston College campus on a Saturday morning and have coffee and muffins for a half hour, catching up with one another about recent events in their schools and in their lives. There always seemed to be plenty of details to keep abreast of—the latest on the district's new literacy or math curriculum, a check-in with a colleague about a troubled pupil we had discussed in a previous session, or a teacher who was in the midst of conflict with her principal about changes in her assignment in the upcoming school year. We kept the size of the seminars small—never amounting to more than 15 participants at their largest—to encourage a climate of mutual trust. We chose settings on campus that were comfortable so that the purpose of knowledge acquisition promoted by a university would not be supplanted by the more imposing and even intimidating aspects of higher education institutions. After establishing a tone of relaxed informality, we then used an eightfold strategy to structure our seminars.

1. Pressing Concerns. We often began with a discussion of *pressing concerns* that we anticipated were widely shared by the teachers. For example, in one year, contract negotiations between the district and the Boston Teachers Union had broken down. After a period in which teachers were on "work-to-rule" (in which the union tells members to abstain from any activities that are not specified in their contracts), teachers went out on picket lines, and a strike was narrowly averted in the 11th hour. Just 1 month later, a rash of youth violence spiked in Boston, culminating in a young man being shot on a city bus while returning home from school in the middle of the afternoon. These incidents provoked extended conversations on the various conflicting messages teachers received about the strike and the dangers facing young people growing up in the central city. On other occasions, more prosaic concerns, such as the district's evolution of collaborative coaching and learning by teacher leaders, provided topics that led to animated conversations.

2. Selective Vulnerability. Next, we moved into a previously chosen topic of *selective vulnerability* from a teacher leader on a question of immediate concern to that person. In some instances, we knew that teachers were struggling with administrators about topics ranging from test preparation to curriculum implementation, to simply the tone of voice used when issuing directives to staff. In other cases, teachers brought forth issues that were entirely within their purview. One lively session began with the question, "I've hidden the pencil sharpener—now what?" in which a teacher opened up for conversation the topic of compromises that we all make when trying to establish a peaceful classroom environment but simultaneously curtail students' freedom of movement.

On other occasions teachers discussed their exasperation at the many factors—from announcements over loudspeakers to disrespectful colleagues to entertaining but educationally useless school assemblies—that cut into their precious instructional time. There is so much to discuss with one another, if only we can create the right collegial environment in which no one has all of the answers and we can be honest about how demanding teaching is today! Much depends upon the tenor of the leadership of a seminar or workshop. Humanistic, mindful leadership should avoid the proclivity to have an answer for every problem, so that teachers can generate their own questions without fear of intimidation or rebuke. By creating an open space of selective vulnerability on professional challenges common to us all, teachers found immediate entry to areas in which they also struggled and shared strategies and responses with one another that they found helpful.

3. Scholarly Research. A third component of the Mindful Teacher seminar concerned a brief presentation and discussion of *scholarly research* on a topic. Here the effort was to expand teachers' awareness of their everyday concerns by informing them of what scholarship indicated on the matter. Our discussions differed from those policy briefs calling for "translational research" (Dynarski, 2008, p. 52) because our assessment has been that scholarship on topics such as literacy instruction, math curricula, and second-language learning often is quite contested, sometimes vehemently so. Yet teachers are often told "research proves that . . .," as if research findings are clear and the consequences for implementation are unambiguous. When teachers receive such messages, their own diverse and contradictory experiences are rendered suspect.

Teachers need to know that scholarship provides clear answers to their questions in some areas—inconsistent messages to students about classroom management are commonly disastrous, for example—but ambiguous findings in others. A blending of phonics and whole language is recommended by most reading experts, for example, but the nature of the blending is open to interpretation (Snow, Burns, & Griffin, 1998). That interpretive space is where teacher professionalism should enter in, with on-the-ground knowledge of the individual children in one's classroom and their complex and evolving personalities. Policymakers can dictate the kinds of instruction teachers should deliver all that they want, and some policymakers do. In the end, however, there is no bypassing the need for careful discernment of complex issues and the continual honing of reflective judgment that is *informed* but not *driven* by the available research.

4. Formal Meditation. Fourth, we practiced *formal meditation* to calm and concentrate the mind as a regular part of seminar activities. Most of our participants had received no formal meditation training previously, and although they were curious about meditation, it is of course unusual for teachers to sit silently together with their eyes closed or focused on a midrange object a few feet away from them. Yet once the teachers settled into the idea that meditation was not part of a cult and the seminar leaders had no covert agenda of proselytizing, they came to cherish this time for peace, quiet, and focused contemplation.

There are many different forms of meditation. In one form of meditation, an individual simply tries to clear and calm one's mind, for example, by following one's breath and continually returning to it when one finds one's attention drifting away with preoccupations. Here it is a matter of acknowledging the mind's tendency to become entangled in past regrets and future plans that, if unchecked, can deplete our experience of the present moment.

With another form of meditation, one first calms one's mind by focusing on the present moment. One then turns one's attention to a matter of concern and considers the issue from a calm and nonjudgmental frame of awareness. Attaining this kind of equanimity was helpful when teachers were grappling with a challenging student, for example. We used both forms of meditation in our Mindful Teacher seminars.

5. Small-Group Work on Psychological Intrusions. Fifth, after meditation, teachers often broke into small groups of dyads or triads to reflect upon *topics that intruded upon their consciousness* while meditating. On those occasions participants made a mental note of the intrusion during meditation before returning to the contemplative practice. Why was it that difficulties with one particular child would intrude, for example, just when a teacher had calmed her mind by following the rhythm of her breath? We let the participants know that this is the nature of the mind. It wanders. It is restless. No moral judgment should be passed, because a wandering mind is a human mind. After a given amount of time—say, 20 minutes or a half an hour—participants then would share with the group at large the reflections that came to the surface through meditation.

By using these simple contemplative practices, a whole host of topics bloomed forth as generative themes for the group. These came from any number of directions. One teacher resented the manner in which her colleagues took advantage of her reputation as an effective disciplinarian; these colleagues would send disruptive pupils into her classroom, without a single word of warning or explanation, because they couldn't or wouldn't deal with the pupils directly themselves. Another teacher struggled with a paraprofessional who was assigned to her; the paraprofessional, on bad days, treated the children in her care with thinly veiled contempt. A third teacher was so preoccupied with the misconduct of a child with severe behavioral disorders in her classroom that she hardly could sleep at night in anguish over what the next day would bring.

The purpose of this component of the Mindful Teacher seminar was to examine each of these dilemmas in a situation of calm and compassionate reflection. We wanted to see the dilemmas for what they truly were. In one case, it might be reflections of a teacher having reached her breaking point with students who acted out. In another, the dilemma might have to do with the teacher's perceived lack of support from the school administration. Another teacher was feeling the pressures of high-stakes testing.

We inquired into these familiar, everyday, intensely experienced dilemmas in all of their breadth and depth to provide mutual support for each other and to explore new possibilities for teaching and learning together. As indicated earlier, we used a language of "befriending our questions" that arose through meditation and interactions in dyads and triads to create an ambience of open-minded inquiry and reflection.

It was important for participants to be able to express alternative conceptions of their teaching that contradicted the points of view of the seminar leaders. We had some participants who were focused on raising pupil achievement with the goal of narrowing the achievement gap between Hispanic and African American students on the one hand and white and Asian pupils on the other. To reach their goals, they embraced instructional practices based on data-driven decision making that have been criticized earlier in this volume. If the seminar truly was to be a professional setting, then it was of the greatest importance that every participant could be free to reflect on how they best could teach their pupils. For it is often not so much the practices in and of themselves as it is the ways that they are introduced or implemented in a particular classroom or school context that is beneficial or problematic (Payne, 2008).

6. The Tuning Protocol. As the group evolved over time, we found that these first five stages of the seminar described thus far—discussions of current developments in the school district, selective vulnerability from a teacher leader, the sharing of scholarly research, mindfulness meditation, and small-group discussion and clarification—often were not enough for the more complex and troubling issues that arose. On such occasions we elected to use a sixth component—the *tuning protocol* developed by educators affiliated with the Coalition of Essential Schools—to look more deeply into our concerns (McDonald, Mohr, Dichter, & McDonald, 2007, p. 63). This protocol allowed us to slow down and to deepen the course of a morning's discussions with more extended attention to one particular problem in detail.

How does the tuning protocol work? In the context of the Mindful Teacher seminar, one participant with an especially pressing concern would volunteer to share the issue with the whole group in depth. The participant would first describe the issue while other participants listened silently. A facilitator of the protocol has to make sure that the presenter is not interrupted as the case is first presented. Then participants could ask clarifying questions—not questions of interpretation or speculation—for 15 minutes. Next, participants would discuss their own interpretations of the situation for a half hour, during which time the presenter could not interrupt and comment. Then the presenter would react with thoughts, with other participants forbidden from speaking. Finally, the group would have an open dialogue, followed by a debriefing of the whole activity.

We needed the formal structure of the tuning protocol and the possibilities it opened for rigorous inquiry when dealing with troublesome aspects of change that went to the heart of teachers' understandings of their practice. In the first year of the seminar we had two participants who were both science specialists and beginning teachers at the same elementary school. With no malice intended, both teachers were approached by the literacy coach in the building and urged to have the children keep writers' journals in science. Both teachers were sympathetic to the idea because they believed in interdisciplinary curricula and understood that literacy entails skills that can be stretched across all academic content areas. Still, they found themselves bristling at the implication that the content of science as a discipline, which already receives minimal amount of time in many elementary schools, wasn't just as important as reading and writing.

Yet how can a science teacher—and a beginner at that—respond when one is in an urban school that has to show make adequate yearly progress on literacy and math across student subgroups? The consequences of poor performance on the tests are real. While educators might not like public exposure involved in teaching in a failing school, the stakes are highest for the students. Should one then begin to modify science instruction and curriculum to introduce literacy activities to help the pupils get ready for the reading component of the state test? Or should one hold fast to the notion that there is a certain disciplinary integrity and intellectual cohesiveness to science that must be preserved and transmitted, and that, given the short time one has the children each week, exploring the wonders of photosynthesis, electricity, and meteorology shouldn't be truncated to make way for test-preparation activities for another discipline altogether?

Our Mindful Teacher seminar was not a venue for *solving* such questions. It *was*, however, a setting for *reflecting* upon them. Our experience was that such reflection, in and of itself, was experienced by the teachers as *emancipatory*. Contrary to many studies on teaching, we experienced that teachers *did* want to theorize about their activities. The teachers were not anti-intellectuals who only wanted to be told what to do: They wanted to make sense of their situations.

When there is a relentless push for practical solutions, it can be a great relief to understand that, in point of fact, there often are *only* imperfect pathways forward out of complex dilemmas. Given a supportive collegial setting, teachers could in general see past simplistic oppositions of right and the wrong to arrive at more complex judgments about resolutions that would work in some contexts but not in others. This complex process of decision making and reflection was not viewed as a default option when nothing else worked, but rather as the epitome of the complex and indeterminate art of teaching itself.

In the case just presented, a mindful and selective incorporation of a literacy coach's recommendations, while preserving the core integrity of the discipline of science, was warranted. The teachers needed to preserve professional integrity yet be alert to a policy context that could lead to trouble for the school if one is overly principled or rigid. Here the play in the system has to be explored with nuance, skill, and sensitivity to children's own interests and needs. Respectful engagement with one's colleagues—responding not with anger or pride, but with a questioning approach addressing how teachers as colleagues can best meet children's needs—raised the tone of inquiry to a higher, more intellectual and ethical level of sustainable collegial learning and future professional growth.

7. Debriefing. The seventh component of the Mindful Teacher seminars involved an *extended debriefing and exploration of opposing themes and experiences.* Here we were careful to discourage any and all forms of groupthink that often bedevil not just teachers' work cultures, but those of virtually any professional setting (Campbell, 2005; Lima, 2001). One important manner for signaling respect for the integrity of multiple points of view is that the seminar leaders early on made a point of noting that we ourselves have areas of disagreement and contention with one another about contemporary education. For instance, one of us had conducted years of research on community organizing and its potential for improving parental involvement and urban education, whereas the other had experienced the frustrations of having only three parents out of a class of 20 students showing up on parents' night. One of us liked the state's standardized tests because of the way they held all children to a common standard and provided a focus for instruction, whereas the other was more critical, worried that excessive attention to the tests was distorting a broad and inclusive curriculum that would allow all children multiple points of entry to learning.

Given the power differences that exist between a university professor and an elementary school teacher, it was important for seminar participants to see that a teacher could feel comfortable challenging a professor to use more down-to-earth language or to be not only abstract but also practical. Likewise, the theoretical challenges that a professor could suggest not only to act, but also to think about one's actions, also contributed to the group discussions.

At times the disagreements between the two seminar leaders became animated arguments with vigorous challenges to each other's ideas and our reasons for holding them. Seminar participants joined in during these debates, sometimes favoring interpretations that neither of us held, such as following district mandates from a sense of respect for authority rather than testing them inwardly in light of one's experience and the evidence. One especially raucous session involved split opinions on Charles Payne's *So Much Reform, So Little Change: The Persistence of Failure in Urban Schools* (2008). We had chosen it for book study, and whereas half of the teachers in the seminar loved it for its honest description of bureaucracy and cronyism, the other half worried that it would discourage young teachers from even considering a career in urban schools.

Each of us tried to convey to the seminar participants that although we held different points of view, we did not want to make fetishes of them, and neither should they. The challenges of urban schools today are multilayered. Teachers are thrown into the midst of institutions that are at the intersection of a host of unresolved societal contradictions. Even if teachers disagree with many dimensions of U.S. public education, as part of their job requirements, they often have to uphold certain aspects of schools, including those that they dislike. The same could be said of principals, central office staff, superintendents, and school board members. When problems are complex, the solutions must be also. This means that educators need to get smarter and to develop more stamina. We need to open our minds to think more courageously, exploring solutions for which there is an evidence base. Above all, we need to deepen our opportunities for further learning and growth with one another.

8. Mindfulness Assignments. The intention of our seminars never was only to be reflective in the meetings themselves, but rather to practice mindfulness throughout one's personal and professional lives. To enhance this goal, we gave participants tasks that we described as "mindfulness assignments." Some examples are as follows:

- We usually are preoccupied with some students in our classrooms and less aware of others. Your assignment is to shift your focus to one or two of the students in your classroom who have been most marginal to your awareness and to write about how that changes your relationships with the pupils.

- We have worked in our seminars to befriend our questions and to use them as points of departure for sustained inquiry and reflection. Find ways to embed similar practices into your classroom to enable your students to understand the power and validity of their own questions and how they can drive and enrich their learning.
- Examine an area that troubles you in your classroom or school—a new curriculum, a vexed relationship with a colleague, or a standoff with a pupil that threatens to erode further—and explore ways that you could use mindfulness practices to change how you are viewing the problem and to shift its dynamics.

These assignments then provided bridging activities linking one seminar meeting to the next. They allowed knowledge to accumulate, to become connected to available research, and to become more intricate over time.

WORKING WITH TEACHERS' GENERATIVE THEMES: 10 CLUSTERS OF QUESTIONS

Using the eightfold organizational structure just described, the following 10 *clusters of questions* surfaced in the Mindful Teacher seminars:

- What should I do when my beliefs conflict with new mandates? How should I act when it seems that the district administration is not aware of the on-the-ground realities of my classroom and school?
- How can I preserve my sense of dignity when I am not treated professionally by my principal or other administrators? What possibilities do I have to change the climate in a positive manner by not lashing back reactively but by modeling professional ethics in my own classroom and in my interactions with colleagues?
- How can I bring the demands of my work life under control to preserve a healthy personal life? How can I create boundaries so that my personal life isn't overwhelmed by my professional obligations?

- Why is there so much inequity within and across schools and school systems? Why are some schools, even within urban systems, awash in resources and support, whereas others struggle just to keep a steady supply of toilet paper and soap in the children's restrooms?
- What does it mean to be a teacher leader? How can I help to build support networks for teachers in a way that leads to my renewal rather than burnout?
- What do I need to know about to respond effectively to violence in schools and communities? How can my own way of interacting with children, colleagues, and parents in my building contribute to a more peaceful, compassionate environment?
- What adjustments do I need to make to develop the stamina to stay in teaching over the long term? How can we best handle our emotional reactions when we sense that our daily work realities as teachers are not well represented or served?
- How can I remain mindful of different perspectives and detached from my own point of view, especially when I find myself becoming judgmental or ideological in the press of events? If I accept that the creation of new categories is an important part of mindful learning, how can I stretch my thinking beyond compliance into a new kind of learning that is both more rigorous and creative?
- How can I develop positive relationships with parents and other community members who are important constituencies in my school? How can I contribute to changing historical patterns of mistrust and even animosity to social trust and compassion?
- What factors should we be aware of when we differ from our students in regard to race, class, culture, home language, or gender? What assumptions might we be making or what stereotypes might we hold that have been transmitted to us by the broader culture, and how can we teach against stereotypes in our classrooms while still respecting state standards and curriculum frameworks?

Six Anchoring Illustrations

Teachers helped one another to work through these 10 clusters of questions throughout our seminars. *Six anchoring illustrations* will now be presented to provide examples of the kinds of cases teachers brought to seminar discussions. These are cases that the teachers themselves selected to illustrate the nature of their everyday challenges. Through discussion and collaborative writing of the cases, the teachers endeavored to show how mindful engagement with their colleagues could help, at least partially, to address them.

Each of the cases is related to one or more of the clusters of questions in the previous bulleted list. These are concrete cases involving practical matters of teaching and learning. They show how mindful teaching, although not an elixir for problems that have historical and institutional features that go far beyond a given teacher's capacities to resolve, can provide a valuable point of departure for understanding and addressing the problems. They show how what might appear to be a fairly abstract theory of mindful teaching can make specific, actionable contributions that address the conflicted nature of teachers' contemporary workplace demands.

Olivia Jones: Teaching the Civil Rights Movement. Olivia Jones[1] knew that she wanted to be a teacher from a very early age. Her parents brought her up in a loving religious environment that left her with a strong social responsibility to learn about and care for others. She attended an urban public school system in New York, in which she experienced a positive diverse environment, and decided that she wanted to work in a similar secondary school. She started teaching right after college at an urban school and soon entered a master's degree program geared for urban teachers at Boston College. After completing her program, she was hired at a middle school in Boston.

Olivia shudders when she remembers her early teaching experiences, which she describes as "insane! When I went to Clark, it was almost as if I had never taught before. We were constantly breaking up fights, and the teachers were always being ridiculed by the principal. My kids have nothing. My school is like a dumping school. We have some parents who try their hardest and are willing to help, and we have others hang up on us when we call them."

She was also stunned by how the administration and the faculty were divided: "We were not unified. Our principal was a dictator, and teachers shut down pretty quickly. It was so crazy that first year. Only at the end of it did some of the teachers begin calling each other by our first names." Slowly, a small group of teachers began to cohere and to help one another.

Olivia knew from her own experiences and from research on urban education that it is important to have a schoolwide culture that holds the children to high standards. She knew that under the leadership of Superintendent Tom Payzant, the BPS had already endorsed a model of whole-school improvement plans to help to create such cultures. In her own building, however, there really was no common culture shared among the faculty; the teachers were utterly "balkanized" (Hargreaves, 1994, p. 213). The only thing they shared in common was their fear of their principal and the trust of a small group of colleagues, usually based in the same team and working with the same children.

One of Olivia's major crises as a teacher occurred when she planned a large interdisciplinary unit on the history of the civil rights movement, with guest speakers, films, and a variety of readings. She found that her students were galvanized by the readings, and she hoped to inspire and impress her principal by inviting him into the classroom to see what her pupils had accomplished. She was shocked when the principal appeared apathetic in regard to the unit and instead insisted on making sure that she was teaching the students to pass the Massachusetts Comprehensive Assessment System (MCAS).

In many ways, the Mindful Teacher seminar was designed to reach out to and support teachers like Olivia. When she first joined the seminar, accumulated wounds of years of intimidation and isolation had taken a toll. She provided harrowing descriptions of verbal abuse that teachers endured at the hands of her principal. She needed a safe environment in which she could describe how bizarre it was to have her principal do a teaching evaluation of her when he couldn't even spell her last name properly and virtually never was seen in her part of the building except when a crisis occurred or when conducting teacher evaluations.

At the same time that it was important for Olivia to describe the climate of fear and oppression in which she worked every day, it was also important for us as seminar leaders to return to the concepts of mindfulness that provided the conceptual undergirding of our seminars. What processes occur that lead idealistic educators who enter the profession with all kinds of exalted hopes to become worn down with the passage of time and to end up as authoritarian administrators who view their colleagues as enemies rather than as allies? Do teachers understand and appreciate the anxieties of parents and the public in general to know that their children are achieving academically, and do they appreciate the contributions of accountability, however defined or implemented, to improve pupil learning? What resources do teachers have to persuade administrators and the public that they really do have children's best interests at heart, and that they endorse the goal of high levels of academic achievement that everyone wishes for our young people?

The Mindful Teacher seminar supported Olivia not just by validating her integrity as a professional and a human being, but also by moving her through our eightfold structure in a way that enabled her to break out of her defensive formations to acknowledge the complexity of the social situation in which she was working. By starting with an examination of the vulnerabilities of teachers, she could see that she was not alone and that her own private problems as an educator had a social dimension that was in many ways beyond her control. By looking deeply into the multiple pressures placed upon her principal, she could come to understand his exasperation and challenges in trying to keep his building from spinning out of control. A brief excursus on the intersection of race, poverty, and social control in the urban schools could help to remind us that the problems of urban education have not originated with this principal and that American society has failed at providing an equitable education to our most disadvantaged children.

Shortly after discussing Olivia's situation, we invited two former upper-level administrative leaders from the BPS to speak with us at the Mindful Teacher seminar. The administrators explained their own challenges in attempting to provide adequate support and oversight of the 150 schools in the district—a task easier said than done when one considers the continual emergence of crises that demand immediate attention and subvert the kind of careful, long-term planning needed to create systemic change. They expressed their frustrations with union guidelines that make the removal of poor teachers such a long and onerous process that administrators generally decide to put up with the worst teachers rather than remove them.

They also reminded the teachers that many of the reforms that had been piloted by the BPS—the funding of literacy, math, and curriculum coaches, for example, or the institutionalization of collaborative coaching and learning—were designed not to oppress teachers but to provide them with additional resources to reflect upon and improve their teaching (Reville, 2007). From their side of the table, so to speak, they experienced in a negative form what Linda Darling-Hammond (1990, p. 339) has described as "the power of the base over the top," discovering that some teachers rejected out of hand even the most rigorous of new research findings in favor of traditional practices that had failed with students in the past and would continue doing so in the future.

By hearing from the two former administrators and learning of their own frustrations at simply not having enough time to improve learning in a vast network of different schools, the teachers began to soften their criticisms of administrators. They came to appreciate that administrators, too, were exasperated at working in an underfunded school system with many bureaucratic guidelines in place that were a disservice to pupils. The duality of "us against them" began to be replaced by a more complex understanding of a whole range of forces that lead to depersonalization and dehumanization, with no obvious single force or factor available to play the role of villain.

The contribution of the Mindful Teacher seminar in this instance was not a direct intervention that raises test scores, but rather the creation of a more multifaceted approach to the social dynamics of an urban school that allows a more empathic, open-minded spirit of inquiry and problem solving to emerge. The seminar cannot, of course, stop an administrator from intimidating teachers—but it *can* provide teachers with a new frame for understanding their administrators, for discussing skillful and unskillful ways of working with them, and for discovering common ground. An in-depth study of the civil rights movement should not be distorted to become just another topic for test preparation, but the opposition between subject-knowledge depth and test preparation may be more fluid and negotiable than sometimes appears to be the case.

Olivia's experiences demonstrate the importance of guided assistance when negative experiences lead teachers to resort to patterns of defensiveness that obscure ongoing inquiry and the search for new categories of meaning-making that can overcome apparent oppositions. In many ways, her experiences illuminate the salience of Ellen Langer's understanding of mindfulness as openness to new experience and the engendering of new categories of understanding. With such greater mindfulness, the paralyzing "Ingroup Virtue/ Outgroup Vice" polarity that Charles Payne (2008, p. 26) has documented among urban teachers can begin to be addressed as a major impediment to raising social trust in the urban school environment. Needless to say, such open-mindedness and introspection among teachers can only be successful if it is matched by similar attributes among administrators.

Megan Mahoney: From Meditation to Classroom Quiet Time. Another form of mindfulness, with reference to contemplative practices, can be found in the experiences of Megan Mahoney, a special educator in the BPS. Megan found the practice of meditation in the Mindful Teacher seminars to be calming after a week of stressful instruction. In her journal, she described the value of meditation:

> When I first joined the Mindful Teacher project 2 years ago, I had no idea what to expect. I knew that I would be meeting with other teachers who were placed in urban settings to share and reflect upon our experiences. . . . As we began, I have to admit that I was quite skeptical of meditation. We meditated at each of our meetings, and I found myself beginning to look forward to, and appreciating, the time that was set aside for meditation at each of our Mindful Teacher meetings. I truly enjoyed that time to myself. I felt free to think freely and uninterrupted and could truly begin to reflect on my students, my classroom, my teaching, and my own personal life. As a teacher, there is so little time set aside to quiet your mind. At times I was able to really clear my head, or to wrap my mind around a different issue in my classroom at this time.

We invited participants to practice concentration meditations to calm their minds and then to turn their attention to their classrooms to observe those topics that were preoccupying them. In Megan's case, after an early meditation session together, she shared that she was preoccupied with two boys in her class who were especially demanding of her time. "The more I worked with one who had special behavior issues," she commented, "the worse he became. I went so far as to keep him after school to give him individual help. It didn't make the changes I thought it would." Several other teachers chimed in, sharing that they felt especially guilty toward well-behaved students who received less attention than those who were acting out and disrupting instruction.

As a special educator working in a substantially separate environment with a small group of students identified with a range of learning disabilities, Megan experienced high levels of frustration daily. She had learned in her teacher education program that she needed to be acutely aware of the alternative needs of children with learning disabilities that so often are coupled with social and emotional challenges. By identifying those needs, Megan knew it was her responsibility to personalize instruction for the pupils by capitalizing on their previous knowledge bases and skills.

Yet Megan also knew that special educators had fought long and hard to ensure that children with special needs would no longer be exempted from state examinations. Advocacy groups argued that the on-the-ground reality of schools simply was that unless children were tested, they were not going to receive any concentrated attention. This especially became the case the more that high stakes were attached to test results.

This lack of attention to the testing of students with learning disabilities became such a major social justice issue that groups such as the National Council for Learning Disabilities lobbied Congress so that the No Child Left Behind Act would mandate that *all* children would be assessed on state tests. Students with autism, dyslexia, or Down syndrome would be tested just like everyone else. Consequently, Megan found that she needed to norm her instruction so that her students—who represented the school's subcategory of special needs—would achieve proficiency on the MCAS tests, thereby securing adequate yearly progress.

These policy changes had direct ramifications for Megan's classroom. When she first began teaching, the majority of her time with her pupils was spent on remediation. At that time her students had to take MCAS examinations, but because there was no high-stakes accountability in regard to the results, they received little attention from the administration. No Child Left Behind required that special education students receive greater attention as one subgroup whose results would be disaggregated from those of the school as a whole. To help prepare her students for the rigor of the state test, Megan now spent less time on remediation and more time trying to keep up with the pacing guides, which included challenging grade-level assessments.

Megan found classroom management to be the most challenging during the assessment periods. Some students would break down and cry. Others would storm out of the classroom. Megan tried to reassure the students that they could indeed do the test, but inside her heart was breaking when she saw that many of the children only were capable of signing their names on the examinations, leaving all of the subsequent sections blank.

It was during one of these critical incidents that, with the teachers in the seminar, we developed our own mindful interventions in the spirit of Ellen Langer. We decided that we would try to direct our attention to a student in our class who was most on the periphery of our awareness and away from the students who demanded disproportionate amounts of attention. When Megan began trying to regulate her behavior in this manner, she immediately found that it was challenging in respect to one of her boys: "It is difficult to ignore attention-seeking behaviors from across the room," she wrote in her journal. "The key seems to be keeping the other students from getting involved in his behavior." Yet she was willing slowly to shift her attention in a deliberate manner to the other students who were trying to learn. Although it took time and careful scaffolding, the problematic student ultimately benefited by becoming more self-regulating. At the end of this small intervention, Megan wrote, "Hopefully this withdrawal of constant attention over time will increase his chances of success in the following years."

Megan was especially concerned that her students who acted out most were having a negative impact on other students, both by distracting her and by indicating that disrespect was an effective way to gain the teacher's attention. Her solution to the problem was to increase the attention that she gave to quieter students and to build "quiet time" into the day when students could "reflect about the day or about issues the kids were having." She wanted the students not only to think about classroom activities, but also to think about their own thinking and to observe how it changed during the course of a day. "Lately, after a big outing or test or sometimes when the students look stressed, we stop and have 10 minutes of quiet reflection time," she reported.

Although teaching is never easy and predictable, Megan found that by redirecting her attention, and by building an atmosphere in her classroom that created a more calm and attentive environment, her class became more manageable and focused. Intriguingly, it was *not* a matter of doing more in the sense of preparing more and better activities. Nor was it a matter of aligning her instruction with tests, or using data to drive her decision making, or any of the other reforms that are most discussed in policy circles today.

The simple opening into a calm time that enabled students to process the events of the day and to be more attuned to what was going on inside and outside of them seemed to make the difference. "As this past month has progressed it is clear that by consciously shifting my attention away from the one student who consumed my thoughts both in and out of school that I was able to create a shift in my classroom community dynamic," she wrote. "That quiet time meant more to the students than talk time with me."

For Megan and her students, the quiet revolution of mindful teaching was an important antidote to incessant busyness and reactivity. Slowing down in this case is not an indulgence but a correction that provides a buffer against external pressures and demands. Megan benefited in the process, and so did her students.

Renee Simmons: Safety as a Precondition for Learning. Renee Simmons had a child when she was in her third year of undergraduate studies at Northeastern University. At the time she was preparing to be an elementary school teacher with a minor in special education. However, after the birth of her son, she realized that she was not going to be able to continue with her studies. With deep regret, she dropped out to get a full-time job at a local YMCA. Once her son turned 4 and entered the BPS, she continued working a full-time job and struggled to make ends meet. Eventually, with the support of her community members, including those from her church, Renee was able to complete her degree in education and obtain a position at a public school in Boston in 2003.

Renee began as a kindergarten teacher in her first year. She was switched to the 5th grade in her second year (because of her low level of seniority). She became a 1st-grade teacher in her third year. The switching was hectic, but Renee understood it was necessary because of declining enrollments in the neighborhood where she worked. She became skilled at starting all over again with lesson planning each year, and her principal appreciated her flexibility. Something else concerned Renee more than the overwhelming demands of switching grades, learning new curriculum, and designing new lessons. These she could manage. What bothered her the most, however, was the disconnection between the school in which she worked and the communities from which the children came.

From Renee's perspective, she sees a school district in which the majority of teachers are unfamiliar with (and too many lack curiosity about) the community conditions BPS pupils experience. Because she lives in the same section of the city as many BPS students, she knows firsthand about the unsettling conditions of inner-city neighborhoods. She knows what it is like to wake up after a restless night, when police helicopters circle overhead with their search lights on. She knows that the police potentially help with crime protection, but they also awaken sleeping children and contribute to an atmosphere of round-the-clock anxiety and surveillance. And she knows tragedy not only when young people are attacked and even killed as gang violence spins out of control, but also the broader impact when children are afraid to play outside, and even being on a city bus in the middle of an afternoon is no shelter from senseless shootings and robberies.

At one point, teachers at Renee's school began hearing story after story from their pupils about incidents of bullying and fights on the school bus as children took the long rides to and from school. Because of Boston's choice model, children can travel all the way across the city. It can make for a bus ride of close to an hour for some of her pupils. It's a long time to sit alone without any supervision or activity other than talking to friends or looking out the window. By listening to the children, Renee gradually was able to piece together many problems that were undermining learning for many of them.

Bored on the buses, and with no adult guidance other than that provided by the driver, older pupils began taunting younger ones to fight one another, with regular altercations and many tears shed before the children arrived to school in the morning. Teachers began hearing about parents who had threatened to kill students who had begun fights with their children on the school buses, and police began reporting incidents of students throwing things out of windows or causing serious injuries to one another as playful jostling turned into serious physical attacks. Problems like these had been occurring for years, but the situation seemed to be spinning utterly out of control.

During our Mindful Teacher seminar meetings, we discussed the division between the schools and the communities that has been a gaping wound in Boston for decades. The infamous school busing crises of the 1970s only exposed a decades-old pattern of racism and social exclusion that led parents of color to suspect the motives of teachers and administrators in the school system. Although the city has struggled to progress, it remains, like all American cities, segregated by race and class.

In our seminar, we asked ourselves how the teachers in Renee's school could best respond to the increasingly chaotic situation on the buses. We learned that the district was had been planning to respond by taking one of the most troubled buses and dividing its pupils into two separate buses. This proposed remedy had potential to solve the problem, but in the interim, one student in Renee's class pleaded with her for protection.

Aware that children really can't concentrate on learning when they are fearful, Renee began riding the school bus with the children from her home in Roxbury to school each day. Renee's presence on the bus immediately changed the atmosphere of anxiety and tension experienced by the children. Because she was known as a strict disciplinarian who was also devoted to the children's well-being, the fighting among the children entirely stopped. The children were able to arrive at school calm and ready to learn.

Unlike Renee, most urban educators do not come from urban environments themselves. Their own backgrounds are suburban or rural, and they are white, not African American. Their point of departure for approaching the urban setting is based on different experiences and identities. In the Mindful Teacher seminars, Renee had a venue for discussing her commitment to advancing social justice as an urban educator and the challenges of living in a community with needs that urban public schools often address imperfectly.

Renee's experiences provided a springboard for the Mindful Teacher seminars for delving into scholarship on community organizing, the achievement gap, and multicultural education. Why is it that so many black boys struggle in school, and why does the achievement gap sometimes widen as young people progress through school? Why is it that decades after the civil rights movement so few teachers of color are in schools today? How can teachers engage their students in discussions of race and class when many of their schools leave these themes unspoken, in spite of students' craving for meaningful and open dialogue?

By asking these questions, seminar participants were searching for ways to understand some of the most complex issues in American society today. Teachers fear that they will be blamed for the achievement gap and that the broader societal failure to address inequities will be placed upon them as individuals and as a profession. They observe that many policies and accountability systems do not really consider out-of-school influences on learning. They know that they face parents in communities of color who observe that their children receive less per-pupil funding and as an aggregate are taught by less qualified teachers than children in suburban districts. In such conditions, no one should be surprised that parents of color come to question the educators' commitment to their children. Race is implicated in these matters, as is class.

These fault lines between predominantly white teaching forces and communities of color first came to a head in northern cities like New York and Boston in the 1960s and 1970s, and their legacies still persist decades later (Formisano, 1991; Perlstein, 2004). To develop an alternative vision of how educators and parents have overcome their mistrust of one another and collaborated, seminar participants read case studies of community organizing (Shirley, 1997, 2002). These provided examples of strategies for developing social capital between educators and communities of color. The case studies provided teachers with hope that their situations could be dealt with like many other problems of the past. They gave the teachers strategies that they could use to transform their schools from outposts of the central office bureaucracy to community centers of pupil achievement and civic engagement.

Jeff Timberlake: From the Nobel Peace Prize to MCAS Camp. Jeff Timberlake had entered a teacher education program that required him to teach for a full year as a student teacher in the BPS. He was assigned to a 2nd-grade teacher who gave him encouragement and support to explore his own ideas and to develop his own signature practices. A high point came for him when he had the opportunity to develop a thematic unit of study on a topic of his own choosing. He consulted the state standards for guidance and then set about creating an interdisciplinary set of lessons about Africa that he hoped would address the Massachusetts social studies standard on leadership.

In the course of his research, Jeff learned about the inspiring political leadership of Dr. Wangari Maathai, a Kenyan human rights activist and environmentalist who launched the "Greenbelt Movement" in Africa that has led to the planting of over 40 million trees to prevent soil erosion (Maathai, 2007). A courageous and independent thinker, Maathai has been imprisoned and violently attacked on multiple occasions for protesting political corruption in her native land. She founded the Mazingira Green Party of Kenya in 2003, became the first African woman to receive the Nobel Peace Prize in 2004, and was chosen to lead the United Nation's "One Billion Trees Campaign" in 2006.

Jeff originally thought that it would be wonderful if his students could plant trees on school property and thus make their own contribution to Dr. Maathai's campaign for sustainable development, but his school had little soil available for planting. He decided to involve students in an art activity of creating their own trees while using readings on Dr. Maathai to teach students about African geography, history, and culture.

Shortly after Jeff had introduced the leadership unit, Dr. Maathai was chosen to be one of eight flag bearers at the 2006 Winter Olympics. One of his students was watching the Olympics with his parents, recognized Dr. Maathai, and was able to describe her leadership to his family. Jeff then wrote a letter to Dr. Maathai, explaining that he was using her in a unit of study and informing her that the students were interested in her work for sustainable development. She wrote back, and he read the letter to the students. "They were pretty blown away by that!" he recalled. "The children felt like they were learning something that wasn't common knowledge to everyone."

At the end of his first year, Jeff received a teaching position at a school that had previously been struggling to meet adequate yearly progress and had received a warning in accordance with No Child Left Behind's policy guidelines. Rallying all of its forces and concentrating on raising achievement, the school subsequently registered test-score gains. Jeff approached the position at his new school with enthusiasm.

Jeff was disturbed, however, to discover that numerous concessions had to be made as part of this drive to support achievement. Outdoor recess had been curtailed in the school, limiting the amount of time his 3rd-graders previously had to exercise and to gain valuable social skills with less adult supervision. Jeff enjoyed the fact that students ate breakfast in their teachers' classrooms but found it frustrating that morning mealtime needed to be accompanied by morning math work. Jeff commented,

> When I first got to the school, I was told by other teachers that due to the most recent MCAS scores, the level of stress was up in the administration, and that in turn was felt by the teachers working there. It was immediately made clear to me that I would not have a lot of autonomy in my classroom. Walkthroughs were done to ensure I was following the schedule and that my content and language objectives were written on the whiteboard. At the time, my feeling was that involving my students with a unit on leadership would not have been supported. The school climate appeared intense. In hindsight, I think some of that intensity was a direct result of the input that I was getting from my peers. There's a process of learning to distance yourself from the chatter going on around you. Still, I remember feeling overwhelmed by the schedule that had been given to me and believed that straying away from it might lead to an unsatisfactory comment in my end-of-the-year teacher evaluation. The majority of my teaching day was devoted to math. I had little, if any, time for one-on-one conferences with my students. I knew this was disadvantageous to my students' growth, but didn't know how to fit those reading and writing conferences into a schedule that was encumbered by the required 90 minutes of math a day.

As the year progressed, Jeff took on additional responsibilities, such as after-school teaching 4 days a week and teaching MCAS Camp on Saturdays. He found himself drowning in the high-stakes environment of testing and accountability, with little restorative time to reflect on his own learning or to adjust his instruction and curriculum to the children in his class. Jeff had entered teaching because he was eager to ignite a love of lifelong learning in young children, but he found himself suffocating in the new school. "It was an emotionally and physically taxing year for me," he recalls. "I had serious questions about my effectiveness as a teacher in urban education. Ironically, I had to take on another commitment—the Mindful Teacher seminar—to allow myself the permission to reflect upon those questions of effectiveness that kept me up at night."

When we shared the Mindful Teacher intervention about focusing on one child who had been on the periphery of participants' awareness, Jeff leaped on the opportunity to dedicate himself to Gregorio, a Salvadoran boy who was always attentive but rarely assertive. He decided to make a book for Gregorio about El Salvador that included a colorful map showing the country's different provinces, a picture of the country's flag, pictures of the national soccer team, and information about El Salvador's Bosque El Imposible National Park.

The following day, during Jeff's guided reading block, he talked to Gregorio. "As a result of trying to meet the demands of my schedule every day, I had inadvertently shifted the focus of my teaching away from the identities of my students and toward checking off things on my list. As I approached this conversation with Gregorio, I felt a certain amount of fear and anxiety melting away." Jeff discovered that Gregorio not only loved soccer but also played the sport with a children's team after school. "After that live encounter with my student, I truly felt reenergized to teach. What's more, Gregorio returned to class the next day with a new energy to learn!"

Jeff is not fluent in Spanish, but he is proficient and able to converse with dominant Spanish speakers. He remembers a change in the mother's demeanor when she dropped off Gregorio at the school in the morning. "She smiled at me," Jeff remembers. Jeff felt proud of the plurality in his classroom; there were students from many countries. He was finding his way back to the idealism that had expressed itself in his project on Dr. Maathai.

Jeff continues to teach because he believes he is good at what he does. Although it is difficult, he finds that he possesses the inner resources and external supports to create an engaging classroom environment while maintaining mindful awareness of the school and its social context. "Honestly, when I find myself overwhelmed by the day or ineffective in my ability to meet the daily pacing guide, I just stop and breathe," he comments. "I remember the importance of my live encounter with that student during my first year of teaching, and I then find new ways to stay connected with the children I have in my classroom now."

Grace Napolitano and Maggie Slye: Mindful Data Analysis. At the
outset of this volume, we criticized data-driven decision making for
reducing the intellectual nature of teaching to simplistic overreactions
to limited and, in many ways, arbitrary assessment measures, particularly high-stakes tests. Jeff's case indicates the distortions that can
occur when testing takes precedence over a caring attitude toward
children. But our criticism of data is misunderstood if one infers that
we are opposed to all forms of data gathering and use. Teachers, like
any other professionals, need to study and use data to inform their
decisions. Just like doctors, lawyers, or engineers, teachers need to
track the impact of their decisions and to make modifications of their
judgments, while staying alert to data sets that do not triangulate with
one another or test-score gains that are spurious because they are not
generalizable.

Two teachers in the Mindful Teacher project exemplify how
teachers can use data to engage others in collaborative learning.
When Grace Napolitano first came to the project, she was exhausted
by an unusually demanding inclusion classroom. For Grace, the
seminars were a lifeline to a world of other professionals who recognized the daunting challenges of teaching today and were eager
to develop their skills to teach to the very best of their ability. The
support that the seminar offered helped her to understand that her
difficulties with behavioral management were not of her own making, but had to do with the manner in which her classroom was
"stacked" with those 4th-grade pupils whose needs were the greatest in her school.

Grace survived the year, but not without wondering whether
she had erred in entering teaching, after many sleepless nights
wracked with anxiety about what the next day might bring. But
behind the emotional toll, she was left wondering how she could
respond quickly and effectively to classroom environments or even
individual pupils who seemed to spin out of control at the smallest
disturbance. She knew that simply complaining about a stacked
classroom, or even pointing out the dubious legality of such pupil assignments in light of federal laws mandating mainstream-
ing and the provision of least restrictive environments, was likely
to garner little sympathy or support from overworked administrators in an understaffed school. For Grace, the solution came
through accepting and capitalizing upon the emphasis on careful

documentation and data gathering that has been so prominent in recent reforms.

One autumn, Grace found herself struggling to teach Miguel, a student who was especially disruptive, whether through singing, humming, lack of body control, or laughing uncontrollably at inappropriate times, such as when a classmate was sharing an idea or reading aloud. Grace thought that Miguel might have attention deficit hyperactivity disorder (ADHD) and contacted Miguel's mother, who set up an appointment with Miguel's doctor to have him assessed. Yet because Grace knew that urban pupils tend to be referred disproportionately for special education services, she was reluctant to pursue this route if she could just discover a way of helping Miguel. But in the interim, what could she do to establish a sense of order and focused attention to learning in her classroom?

Grace worked with her student teacher from Boston College, Marlene Gomez, to study and then to modify Miguel's behavior. In her journal, Grace wrote that the first step of this applied behavioral analysis was simple documentation, so "we broke the day up by subject, then further segmenting each subject into 5-minute increments. This would be our 'data-keeping' sheet. We then took data for 7 days." If Miguel disrupted the class, "we would put a check mark. Sometimes, we would address the behavior; other times we would ignore it depending on how intrusive it was to the class."

What did the data-keeping sheet reveal? Grace "calculated that Miguel missed 930 minutes or 15.5 hours of instructional time over that 7-day period. We looked at where we saw the most checks, and we found that literacy (reading, writing, and phonics) was where we found the highest rate of checks." Grace then worked with Miguel to identify rewards that he would like to earn and were realistic. His rewards included stickers on a chart, a stroll with Grace or Marlene, or time at the end of the day when he could play on a computer, do a puzzle, or play a board game with a friend.

Miguel did not respond immediately to the new incentive system, but after about 2 weeks, his behavior began improving. "He was now able to sit without interrupting the group," Grace wrote. "As a result, Miguel was able to complete his work more efficiently because he had attended to the lessons and understood the objective and material that was being presented." Although Miguel's disruptions continued, they decreased "dramatically, to on average five interruptions per day. This was a significant change in behavior. As a result of this information, we decided that Miguel was not in need of additional services. It appears that Miguel just needs positive attention in a more structured way."

Grace had helped Miguel to develop the social skills and self-control to show proper respect for his classmates, his teacher, and his own learning. Concomitantly, Grace's intervention with Miguel was successful in terms of tracking his literacy gains. In a 5-month period Miguel's Developmental Reading Assessment (DRA) results moved from "preemergent" to "emergent," thereby showing progress.

Maggie Slye, another seminar participant, shows a different dimension of mindful data analysis. Like Grace, Maggie has developed her skills in documenting pupil behavior and learning. In terms of literacy instruction, Maggie's perspective is that the data she has gathered through miscue analyses have revealed that her struggling readers "relied almost entirely on meaning cues, and were stymied by long vowels, digraphs, consonant blends, and diphthongs." Noting that her school, which used Readers Workshop, "did not have a systematic, explicit phonics program," Maggie learned about "a word study program that was explicit, systematic, and included components I felt were essential to lock in letter–sound knowledge, such as decodable text and kinesthetics." Using the new program, she was delighted to discover that "most of my students' reading levels improved by 1.5 years" in the space of a single academic year. "Although there could be countless explanations for their growth, I believe the data I collected during my miscue analyses, and the instructional decisions I made based on that data, substantially contributed to their success."

Maggie confers with her pupils to explain their test results and to provide the support and confidence that will motivate them to excel on the tests. This understanding of the value of data is connected with her professional ethics. Educators must have access to crucial information about their students' lives, both in and out of school, and must know how to use data wisely. In one of her writings for the Mindful Teacher seminar, Maggie explained:

> I think that another important aspect of being a mindful teacher is being aware of the important influences in our students' lives. We collect data on our students' interests to better match them to books that they will love. This, in turn, nurtures a love of reading. We collect data on our students' cultures and traditions to better recognize and honor our

students' individual experiences. This, in turn, fosters a safe, welcoming, and respectful classroom environment that is optimal for learning. Part of collecting data about our students so that we know how to better serve them is creating strong, respectful relationships with their families.

In the examples just presented, Grace and Maggie used data to identify breakdowns in student learning. They then devised action plans of modified instruction and assessment of their students' progress. These improved student learning and produced measurable evidence of improvement. In many ways, this kind of "mindful data analysis" is at the heart of teachers' professionalism. No reform, no matter how perfectly conceptualized, will ever be able to wholly replace this core set of skills and dispositions possessed by educators who are working at peak performance. Mindful teaching and professionalism are unified and integrated in these examples.

Karyn Cirulli: Supportive Changes for Teachers and Children. Karyn Cirulli comes from a small town in Pennsylvania and was overwhelmed by the challenges of working in urban schools. When she first applied for a job in the BPS, she was discouraged. When she arrived for an interview at an agreed-upon time at one middle school, the principal was nowhere to be found. Karyn was excited when she was offered a position as a 1st-grade teacher at an underperforming school in Boston.

Teaching was harder than Karyn had imagined. She found herself challenged on many levels and particularly in regard to the lack of support for students, who had a range of social and emotional needs. Many of her pupils struggled with issues of abandonment, had witnessed abusive relationships, and lived in violent neighborhoods. There was only one counselor in the school, which served over 400 children. The diverse needs of students were inadequately addressed at school, and the press for academic achievement played a role in diminishing reflection about those needs.

Karyn found that she sometimes was not able to teach as she would have liked because her students' behavioral problems impeded her efficacy as an instructor. One year she had an especially difficult situation with a girl named Cecilia whose father had abandoned her and whose mother was in jail. Cecilia was being raised by an aunt, but the Department of Social Services was called upon to monitor her situation when it appeared that the apartment where she lived was unsafe and that her aunt disciplined her in abusive ways.

Cecilia's troubled home life spilled over into her behavior at school. Without a moment's notice, Cecilia would leave Karyn's 1st-grade classroom in the midst of instruction. The protocol in the school was for teachers to contact the principal's office when a child left the classroom. When Karyn did, no one was there to help.

The secretary often was gone from the front office, attending to matters as diverse as handing out Band-Aids, getting copy paper for teachers, or calming down crying children. The principal was fully engaged by tasks such as meeting with parents, observing instruction, or responding to a child in crisis. Sometimes Karyn chased after Cecilia, leaving her classroom unsupervised. At other times she simply decided she could not leave the children in her classroom, thereby allowing Cecilia to wander alone throughout the building. But each and every time that the running occurred, she found herself psychologically split in two, worried about Cecilia and distracted while trying to teach all of the other children who were deserving of her instruction.

When she shared her difficulties with a teacher from across the hallway, she learned that the other teacher also had students with behavioral issues who required constant attention; therefore, she could not help Karyn. She was hopeful when she learned that the central office of the BPS would be sending her school a designated specialist in behavioral management. Unfortunately, the specialist seemed to know little about how to communicate with children like Cecilia. He let Cecilia and other children run the halls because he had no idea of what to do with them.

When Karyn shared this situation with the other Mindful Teacher seminar participants, she heard similar stories. Teachers shared their experiences of dealing with rebellious and violent children with no one else to assist, of altercations with parents, and of children with special needs placed inappropriately in their classrooms without legally required supports in place. Simply learning that many experienced teachers had encountered similar issues was an enormous source of solace for Karyn. She learned that Cecilia's story was about a child in trouble, but it was more than that. It was also about teachers working in a system with inadequate resources for meeting the needs of its students.

Karyn's response to this situation was to set up a "quiet table" where children could be in a safe and semi-private place when there was too much stimulation in the class and they needed their own area. She was delighted when Cecilia responded positively to the table and would use it to write what she was feeling inside. Karyn found that Cecilia wrote about how she missed her mother and how she wished that she could talk with her, go shopping with her, and do all of the normal kinds of activities that girls love to do with their mothers. Karyn tried to encourage Cecilia to believe that one day things would get better, although she herself didn't know what the future would really hold for Cecilia.

Karyn's response of setting up a special writing area for Cecilia did not stop the incidences of her leaving the classroom without permission. But Karyn did notice a real change, because Cecilia began coming back to the classroom of her own accord and then heading straight to the quiet table, where she would write down what she was feeling. Cecilia was beginning to find her own way of dealing with her emotions and impulsiveness, and although Karyn still didn't like it that she would leave the classroom, she came to expect that Cecilia would return on her own—and her expectations were fulfilled.

Karyn's case illustrates the suffering and uncertainty that accompany mindful teaching. Teachers often are in work environments that are not adequately resourced. Administrators are too busy as they respond to a tsunami of pressures of their own. Their fellow teachers have their own classes to look after. Parents are in and out of buildings.

Teachers have to use their professional judgment as they respond to children. Ideally, this is a collective responsibility for the profession as a whole. In reality, professional decisions often have to be made by teachers without the guidance of colleagues.

This loneliness of teaching carries emotional costs for teachers. It is ironic that this most socializing of professions so often places teachers in situations of isolation from their colleagues. It is tragic when one is aware of social scientific research indicating that collective responsibility is essential for organizations to attain peak performance (Hargreaves, Boyle, & Harris, 2014).

For Karyn, it was hard to hold out hope for Cecilia. She herself had always had a very close relationship with her mother and could hardly begin to imagine how much it must hurt to have one's mother in jail—but she knew that it was her personal and professional responsibility to keep hoping in spite of the odds. Simply knowing that there were teachers with similar challenges whom she respected as colleagues and friends in the Mindful Teacher seminar gave her the stamina she needed to persevere and to continue to seek out potential solutions. Truly, one has no choice to stop hoping—for without that hope one becomes part of a problem, rather than a solution, in children's lives.

Learning from the Six Anchoring Illustrations

What do we learn from our six illustrations of what we are calling mindful teaching? If you are a teacher, we anticipate that as you read through the cases, you found ways to identify with each of the teachers. Although we hope that you never have experienced verbal abuse from an administrator as Olivia did, chances are high that you have experienced conflict with administrators and have wondered how you can best advance children's interests in the light of pressing policy demands. Both Megan and Karyn were struggling with ways to shape their classrooms into peaceful and safe environments where pupils could first feel secure and then focus on their learning—certainly a universal concern for educators. Renee's unusual personal engagement—riding a school bus with children to ensure their safe transit—is replicated by tens of thousands of teachers who go far beyond their job descriptions to assist pupils in areas that have little to do with increasing test scores but everything to do with creating environments appropriate for learning. You might find your own aspirations reflected in Jeff's goals and in his quest to promote learning that is meaningful for children. Or you might have found a kindred spirit in Grace or Maggie, who found ways to document pupil behavior and learning that turned problematic situations into positive outcomes. In each case, you may find your own thought processes mirrored in the continual inner reflection of the teachers—that sometimes becomes obsessive in its intensity, precisely because one is dealing with young children who are entrusted to one's care and often have little recourse beyond your decisions about their lives.

Each of these cases, in its concrete manifestations, is to a certain extent bounded by its singularity and specificity. And although anchoring illustrations are important, it is necessary at this juncture to derive general principles from the cases, which, combined with research findings, can help to articulate a theory of mindful teaching and accompanying practices—a task to which we turn in the next chapter.

NOTE

Pseudonyms have been used for selected teachers and schools and for all students to protect confidentiality.

CHAPTER 4

The Seven Synergies of Mindful Teaching

In this chapter we build on our foregoing descriptions and a review of research to elaborate in greater detail what we mean by mindful teaching and to suggest affiliated practices for teachers. By doing so, we seek to assist educators by providing a new conceptual frame for understanding our common challenges and opportunities. In addition, we wish to spark and extend a conversation about mindfulness and its relevance and utility to education. Our discussion is organized around what we describe as *seven synergies of mindful teaching*. Because we do not believe that mindful teaching can address all of the problems currently challenging American education, we describe the limitations of mindful teaching through an elaboration of *three tensions of mindful teaching*.

THE SEVEN SYNERGIES

The term *synergy* originated in medicine and anthropology and conveys the idea that latent resources can be marshaled and released when individual actions are placed in right relationships with others to create a positive dynamism that is renewable and more than the sum of its parts (Benedict, 1934). Charles Payne (2008) has commented that one of the challenges facing urban education is that, in many ways, individual actions actually add up to *less* than the sum of their parts. This is so because many relationships—including those between adults—are riddled with mistrust. If this is the case, then a countervailing set of beliefs and practices that nourish trust and connectedness would seem to be warranted.

Following our seminars and accompanying practices, we reflected upon our findings and attempted to ascertain if there were any underlying patterns or theories of action that could be derived from them to espouse a theory of mindful teaching. We scoured through our tape transcriptions of seminar meetings and our notes from our interviews with seminar participants, and then coded the concerns and solutions that recurred repeatedly. We then clustered those concerns together when they bore a conceptual resemblance with one another, shared our findings with seminar participants, and refined our articulation of each idea through additional elaboration and clarification. Through this process, we identified *seven synergies of mindful teaching* (Figure 4.1).

Why is *synergy* an appropriate term to use? In *Experience and Education*, John Dewey observed that "Mankind likes to think in terms of extreme opposites. It is given to formulating its beliefs in terms of *Either-Ors*, between which it recognizes no intermediate possibilities" (Dewey, 1938, p. 17). Dewey's philosophy of education is based upon the overcoming of such "dualisms" in order to establish harmony and balance in education (Dewey, 1916). In this way Dewey foreshadowed

Figure 4.1 . The Seven Synergies of Mindful Teaching

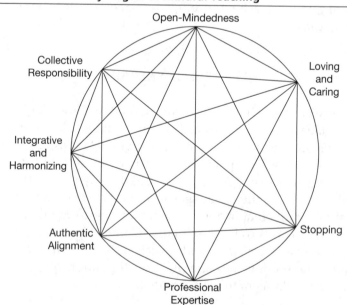

the seven synergies of mindful teaching that we derive from our anchoring illustrations. The importance of open-mindedness, commitment to the whole child, and educators as lifelong learners—the cornerstones of Dewey's philosophy—are reflected in mindful teaching. Not coincidentally, Dewey's philosophy of education met with great popular resonance among Asian scholars, who saw in his effort at overcoming dualisms affinities with their own native traditions of Confucianism, Taoism, and Buddhism (Frisina, 2002).

1. Open-mindedness. The first and most important synergy is a commitment to *open-mindedness*. In our first anchoring illustration, Olivia's perspective grew from that of a defensive teacher into that of an educator who came to understand that administrators suffer under their own sets of pressures, many of which are beyond their control. In the second anchoring illustration, Megan recognized that remediation couldn't be the only instruction required for her special education students and that she needed to mindfully infuse rigorous and complex tasks into their curricula. These illustrations illuminate aspects of Ellen Langer's research (1989, 1997) on mindfulness, which alerts us to habitual modes of acting that can prevent us from being open to new kinds of information that call for new responses.

Is it wrong for teachers to curse, shout at students, and to support parents when they are authoritarian with their children? Most of us would say yes. But education is much more complicated than this. In his research, Pedro Noguera (2008) has discussed his finding that African American students report that they would rather have teachers who hold them to high standards, even if this involves some yelling for emphasis, than teachers who are apathetic and disengaged. In dangerous urban neighborhoods, authoritarian parenting can be more predictive of student success than other approaches because there is such a small margin for error (Benard, 2006).

John Stuart Mill (1867, p. 1) wrote about education: "Of all of the many-sided subjects, it is the one which has the greatest number of sides." Plato's *Republic*, Confucius's *Analects*, and classics of Indian philosophy such as the *Upanishads* and the *Bhagavad-Gita* all embrace the polyvalence and elusive qualities of education. But only rarely do we allow this complexity to emerge. Complexity needs to be enabled, discussed, and debated. Teachers like Jeff need school structures and cultures that will enable this complexity so that they can come to know and teach their pupils better. Being open-minded allows us to engage our pupils as they are now, not just as we might want them to be.

We can't escape sloganeering in education, but too often we let slogan systems substitute for deep reflection. Even our distinctions between alienated and mindful teaching in this book should be called into question. A moment of alienation or disequilibrium can be the prelude for inquiry and for deeper learning about one's assumptions and biases. The centuries-old tradition of Socratic dialogue requires a readiness to doubt and to question one's beliefs.

Many teachers might assume that having a calm and quiet classroom is a necessary part of mindful teaching, but some research on children with attention deficit hyperactivity disorder indicates that playing rock music while performing an academic task helped children to increase their attentiveness to the task (Cripe, 1986). Some children who struggle with abandonment issues find noise and stimulation comforting because they associate silence with the absence of a caretaker (Gil, 2006). So the first ethic of mindful teaching is open-mindedness to the diversity of opinions and experiences.

2. Caring. The second synergy of mindful teaching relates to a disposition of *caring*, or even *loving*, at the heart of teaching. Renee rode the school bus with children from Roxbury because she experienced on a daily basis the connections between the children's learning in school and their environments outside of school. Karyn didn't worry about her "runner" just because Cecilia was distracting other children from learning. She worried about her because the girl was in difficult straits and her longings for her mother elicited the strongest of emotions that were both educational and maternal in nature.

When teachers in our seminar worried that children on individual educational plans were not receiving services legally mandated for them to receive as a result of learning disabilities, they weren't just upset that their schools weren't following protocol. They worried that children were being shortchanged. When teachers in the Mindful Teacher seminar shared how they saw colleagues yelling at children to shut up or insulting their intelligence, they worried deeply that educators were neglecting an ethic of care.

Nel Noddings (1992, 2001) argued that education without a disposition of *caring* could become a hollow and truncated enterprise that will produce skepticism and resistance among learners. Jim Scheurich (1998), in a study of high-achieving schools serving low-income students of color, found that educators' explanations of their success with students often were predicated upon what they rather prosaically described as their *love* of them. Much has been made recently about debates concerning educators' dispositions, with the implication that difficulties about definitions and challenges in operationalizing terms must mean that the terms themselves are illegitimate (Liston, Whitcomb, & Borko, 2007). None of our six anchoring illustrations make sense without recourse to the aspirations that the teachers have for their pupils. Cutting off discussions about these longings—trivializing them as romantic, impractical, or even anti-intellectual—cannot work if education is to manifest itself as a humanistic and humanizing enterprise.

3. Stopping. In an institutional setting in which "innovative overload" and "repetitive change syndrome" have become normalized as routine forms of everyday life, the third synergy of mindful teaching is simply *stopping*.

And then stopping again.

And then stopping yet another time.

It might seem ridiculous to imagine that simply stopping could be described as emancipatory. We are socialized to believe that being busy is a virtue. If this is the case, how could it be that Megan and her pupils had a different experience? What actually was happening when Jeff took the time to sit down with a student to get to know him and his family better? What could stopping mean for a theory of mindful teaching?

Because theory only is effective up to a point, and then experience is more generative, we ask you to try this: *Stop right now.*

Put this book down, assume a posture reflecting your inherent dignity, and close your eyes for a few minutes. Observe calmly and nonjudgmentally the various images, recollections, projects, and longings that surface in your mind. Adapt an inner attitude of compassion toward yourself. Then direct that inner attitude toward your students, starting with those whom you find the easiest to relate to and gradually including those whom you find more challenging. Then allow your attention to return to your aspirations to enable your pupils to reach their full potential. Finally, reflect upon the change in your consciousness at the beginning and at the end of this mindfulness exercise.

With inner peace, more possibilities open up for modifying action than when one is stressed. This finding is reinforced over and over again by research in meditation practices and neuroplasticity (Austin, 1999; Begley, 2007; Siegel, 2007). One can't achieve balance if one is always rushing and engulfed in projects. In such a context, one cannot be sufficiently alert to one's responses to events. Although formal meditation might be an optimal way of stopping, busy teachers cannot always do this, so it is important to recall that "Meditation can be very informal" (Hahn, 2005, p. 16) and can occur in the midst of activities, with the right frame of mind. So the third synergy of mindful teaching is stopping and taking an inner account of what is transpiring, and not allowing oneself to be rushed into actions that one might later regret.

4. Professional Expertise. It is all very well to be open-minded, to be loving, and to stop and think as educators. But what good does this avail students if one does not know the subject matter one is teaching, does not study evidence of student learning, and makes no effort to keep abreast of new research findings? We cannot emphasize sufficiently the fourth synergy of mindful teaching, which is *professional expertise*.

Throughout our seminar discussions, teachers expressed exasperation with colleagues who were not only disinterested in educational research, but who were actively hostile toward those who sought to share it to inform the deliberations of instructional leadership teams. They were enraged by promotions awarded to teachers and administrators on the basis of seniority rather than professional achievements. They felt insulted by philanthropists who patronized them by emphasizing the caretaking aspects of their work rather than their roles in developing students to be critical thinkers, cutting-edge innovators, and global citizens.

Seminar participants developed their professional expertise through multiple venues. Some focused on raising pupil achievement through rigorous drill and assessment activities that they alternated with complex interdisciplinary units that kept their classrooms novel and exciting. Others team-taught teacher education courses at Boston College and opened up their classrooms for research with student teachers, as Grace Napolitano did with Marlene Gomez in one of our anchoring illustrations. Others pursued certification through the National Board for Professional Teaching Standards and used contributions to this book as evidence of continual learning and growth in the profession. Still others sought out learning opportunities outside of their districts to get new ideas to bring back to their students.

Professional expertise is taking on many new forms in schools today. When encouraged by principals through distributed leadership models, it is correlated with gains in pupil achievement (Harris, 2008; Spillane, 2006). When linked with new technologies skillfully and intentionally, it can produce striking learning gains for students with disabilities, and it can do this at the level not just of a single school, but of a whole system (Hargreaves & Braun, 2012; Hargreaves & Shirley, 2012). Andy Hargreaves and Michael Fullan (2012) have articulated a new model of "professional capital" that blends the knowledge of the single teacher (human capital), relationships among teachers (social capital), and the ability of teachers to make good judgments (decisional capital) into a powerful new ensemble.

These are promising points of departure for the profession as a whole. Mindful teaching and learning must not be disconnected from them but integrated and harmonized with them. If all of the work being done today regarding mindfulness in schools does not become anchored in the profession as a whole, this work will not be sustainable. It will suffer the fate of the many promising innovations that have passed in and out of schools because there was insufficient attention given to the needs of the profession as a whole. The quiet revolution of mindfulness cannot be a stand-alone initiative or a project. It must become part of a new way of evolving the teaching profession.

5. Authentic Alignment. Given the complexity of professional expertise, it follows that the fifth synergy of mindful teaching is *authentic alignment*. Educators hear endless amounts today about the need to align their instruction with district standards, professional association standards, and now the Common Core State Standards. The amount of time that goes into establishing charts aligning different standards with one another and with curriculum frameworks and tests is prodigious. In many cases, elementary school teachers are required by their principals, districts, or states to write the instructional objectives for each subject area to be covered—reading, writing, math, science, social studies, and art—on the board at the beginning of each day. They are also required to keep lesson plan books with all of the state standards linked to each activity each and every day. Finally, schools are mandated to teach a certain number of minutes every week for certain subjects.

When viewed as helpful indicators to be considered by novice teachers, such guidelines can provide a useful frame of reference for planning instructional activities. When considered from the point of view of experienced professionals, however, an excessive concern with alignment can rob teachers of opportunities to adjust their instruction to teach students at their actual level of understanding or to create exciting lessons with novel kinds of group structures and purposeful independent study. Teachers need to ask themselves if their teaching approaches are aligned with their own understanding of teaching as a profession, and when dissonance occurs, they need opportunities to reframe their activities.

Recent research by Howard Gardner, Mihalyi Csikszentmihalyi, and William Damon (2001) puts such authentic alignment between ethical conviction and action at the core of professional fulfillment and efficacy. Indeed, without such undergirding ethical principles, it would appear that a profession cannot be sustained, because the core of any professional status relies on implicit social trust among professionals and the public that the professionals are legitimate and acting in the public interest. When professionals neglect ethics, they undermine their own integrity and credibility, and the accompanying public skepticism is a necessary, albeit avoidable consequence.

6. Integration. A sixth synergy of mindful teaching is that it is *integrative*. Michael Fullan (2001, p. 31) has used the phrase "dynamic conservatism" to convey the way in which expert teachers incorporate new practices into their repertoires without abandoning previous strategies. Although some (Cohen, 1990) have decried the manner in which teachers incorporate innovative practices into anterior, more traditional approaches, our perspective is less dualistic. Reformers need to be more respectful of teachers' practices, even those that seem quaint in an age of technological breakthroughs. Some of the older teaching practices that were maintained by Catholic schools while public schools careened from one reform approach to another have been vindicated (Bryk, Lee, & Holland, 1993). Teachers such as Grace and Maggie blended conservative approaches—such as applied behavioral analysis or systematic phonics—with a broader repertoire of progressive pedagogies. Mindful teaching should skillfully blend the old and the new.

7. Collective Responsibility. The seventh synergy of mindful teaching is *collective responsibility*. In high-achieving Finland, there is no term for "accountability" in education (Sahlberg, 2015). The public has rejected the notion because it undermines the shared nature of the enterprise. Significantly, Finland has the smallest achievement gap between the rich and poor of any of the nations measured on the Program for International Student Assessment (PISA) tests (Sahlberg, 2015). The notion that Renee would find herself compelled to ride a school bus so that her pupils would arrive safely to school in the morning would strike the more collectivist Finns as an abrogation of the broader societal obligation to children (Hargreaves, Halász, & Pont, 2008; Hargreaves & Shirley, 2009b, 2012).

We prefer the Finnish understanding of *collective responsibility* to the kind of accountability, or more exactly accountancy, favored by U.S. reformers in the past 30 years. For American educators, and for the broader public as well, this needs to entail a renewal of civic activism—whether through community organizing, social movements, or hybrid public–private partnerships—to reduce the increases in social inequality that have developed in the past quarter century and to improve student learning and well-being (Anyon, 2005; Oakes, Rogers, & Lipton, 2006; Peterman, 2008). Teachers have a special role to play here as those civic professionals who are entrusted with the education of the young (Murrell, 2001). If we are successful, we will be able to move beyond the current period toward what we hope will be a promising new era of poststandardization (Hargreaves & Shirley, 2008).

The seven synergies of mindful teaching—open-mindedness, caring, stopping, professional expertise, authentic alignment, integration, and collective responsibility—provide important principles for developing what we are calling mindful teaching. Because they are synergies and not isolated phenomena, each has to be brought into a mutually supportive relationship with the others if our students are to be well served. They are not a dogma. They could become useless or even destructive if they are communicated in a tone of voice or attitude of dismissal that is wounding and degrading to others.

The synergies of mindful teaching are not about preaching and proselytizing. They address the responsibilities of each and every one of us to adjust our own behaviors in light of our highest principles. And even then the seven synergies are complemented by the triple tensions of mindful teaching.

THE TRIPLE TENSIONS OF MINDFUL TEACHING

The first tension of mindful teaching is *the tension between contemplation and action* (Figure 4.2). To be mindful, one must take time out to become attuned to and reflective about what is transpiring. One can do this through incorporating formal meditation into one's everyday life, through keeping a journal of one's experiences, or through prayer. Students also can be brought into these processes in ways that contribute to a calm and focused classroom environment (Lantieri, 2008; Payton et al., 2008).

Beneficial as these contemplative activities are, in our seminar discussions, teachers continually struggled with issues of time management and the day-to-day pressures of their professional lives in schools. Meditation CDs that we gave the teachers were received appreciatively, but with the press of events they would go unused by several of the teachers, only rarely becoming part of formal daily practices. When teachers like Olivia, Renee, and Jeff took on extra projects and tasks that truly served their pupils, that extra time took away from restorative time they needed to shelter and attend to their private lives. Teachers would promise themselves that they would stop work each evening by 7 p.m. but still be going for hours afterward.

Figure 4.2 . The Triple Tensions of Mindful Teaching

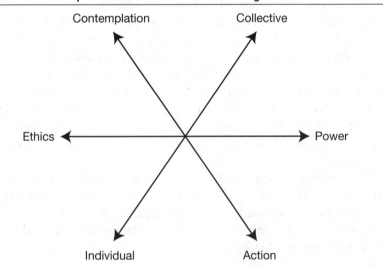

As seminar leaders, we did not know how to resolve the tensions that teachers experienced between the needs of their pupils and their own needs for well-rounded private lives. Many reformers would argue that of course the needs of the pupils come first—but then the same reformers seem puzzled by the horrific rates of teachers leaving the profession. Too many of our seminar discussions came to involve questions of how much longer individuals could remain in the urban classroom. Our role became that of compassionate allies who sought to establish a balance between the needs of the pupils for learning and the needs of the teacher for a profession that invites not 3 years of idealism followed by burnout and exit but, instead, long-term sustainable growth and fulfillment.

The second tension of mindful teaching is *the tension between ethics and power*. Mindful ethics require us to treat others as their own ends and not as instruments for securing our own status or privilege. Here is a point of convergence between Western and Eastern ethics, as expressed, for example, by Immanuel Kant's categorical imperative on the one hand and the Lotus Sutra on the other. As teachers, we need to continually review our decisions and the manner in which we enact them in terms of their contributions to an atmosphere of deep respect and compassion for others. We need to know when to speak up to advocate for our pupils when they do not have the power to advocate for themselves.

One incident in the life of one of our seminar participants is illustrative here. Frank is a 3rd-grade teacher who works in an elementary school in which the children only have 20 minutes of recess per week—and this itself is contingent upon the children demonstrating good behavior and completing all of their homework on time. Many of Frank's children live in neighborhoods that have experienced youth violence in recent years, so some of their parents do not allow them to play outside when they are home from school. They thus have few opportunities to move their bodies about either at home or at school. Emboldened by Mindful Teacher seminar discussions about ethics and advocacy, Frank spoke up at a school staff meeting and argued for more recess time for the children each week. The next morning his principal showed up in his classroom unannounced to conduct an assessment of his teaching.

Frank learned that advocacy for students by teachers can lead to heightened surveillance of teachers by administrators. Yet this second tension exists because an excessive concern with ethics can lead to disengagement from politics. If one is overly moralistic and neglects to acknowledge the realities of power, one can withdraw from the public space altogether, disdaining it as inherently suspect and almost beneath one's dignity. Such a stance is dangerous in any democracy, which depends upon civic engagement to enhance worthy goals related to social justice and human rights. Our project was grant funded, which was not so important in regard to the small stipends it provided teachers but enormously significant in terms of the institutional imprimaturs of Boston College and the Boston Public Schools. Making sure that others outside of Boston knew about the grant through a website (www.mindfulteacher.com), conference presentations, and even this book itself also was important to nourish our ongoing learning as a professional community and to enable others to engage with and critique our work.

The *third tension of mindful teaching is the tension between the individual and the collective*. Teachers are needful of colleagues who will support us during tough times and challenge us when we display errors in judgment that could range from speaking harshly to a child or acting rudely to a parent or another colleague. Ideally, we are all constantly involved in providing one another with mutual support. Yet could it be the case that educators sometimes are subject to groupthink, and that in our praiseworthy goals to be supportive of our colleagues, we sometimes put this ahead of our students' interests and needs?

An important body of research (Campbell, 2005; Lima, 2001) indicates that this is indeed the case, documenting the ways in which educators are conflict averse, preferring the solace of silence to the experience of conflict in the face of injustices. This unprofessional culture of looking the other way—even in the face of egregious injustices to children—has to be engaged directly and overcome. It is too much to put this responsibility onto the backs of single individuals; it must be viewed as a collective responsibility in which professional associations and teacher unions protect dissidence. Therefore, even though an important part of mindful teaching entails valuing calmness and concentration, mindful teaching cannot mean passivity or acquiescence in contexts of injustice. It must call forth civil courage and even bold confrontations.

For many, mindfulness seems to denote inner equilibrium and tranquility. How can this be reconciled with the need to challenge injustices? Crucial here is the spirit and tenor of the confrontations. These must be guided at all times by an ethic of care for one's students above all, but also for others who may feel they are being unjustly criticized. Here is where an ethic of care must be directed not only to students, but also to one's colleagues. Allan Yellup (2013) is one English principal who has modified the government's slogan of "Every Child Matters" to "Every Person Matters" so that all staff are included in a caring school community. It is precisely when we are most motivated by high moral purpose that we can be most prone to dehumanizing others with opposing perspectives. It is for this reason that the road to hell has been paved, stone by stone, with good intentions gone awry.

CODA

The seven synergies of mindful teaching provide purpose, direction, and cohesion to mindful teaching as a set of pedagogical principles and practices. The triple tensions, however, remind us that those synergies cannot pretend to be prescriptive in all situations and contexts. Schools will continue to struggle with abused and abusive administrators and children whose parents are depressed, in jail, or on drugs. School funding streams will go up and down in response to economic booms and busts. Promising innovations, even when they yield excellent results, will be phased out when foundation heads change and new leaders want to put their own imprint on the programs they are funding. Even in well-funded schools with talented educators and strong community support, the very frailty and unpredictability of the human condition will lead to pupils who drop out, staff who quit in the middle of the school year, and administrators who are frustrated by seemingly intractable problems with teachers and children. For all of these reasons—and for many more—we need something more than mindful teaching. We need *mindful teacher leadership*—the subject of our next chapter.

CHAPTER 5

Mindful Teacher Leadership

One major challenge for teacher leadership was articulated many years ago by Michael Huberman (1993), who found that when teachers reflected on their careers at the stage of retirement, those who reported the most fulfillment were those who had evaded involvement in larger school reform initiatives. Those with the most frustration were those who had tried to change system-level policies and had been thwarted in their efforts. This finding subsequently has become known as the "Huberman paradox" (Little & Bartlett, 2002), and its ramifications have troubled teacher leaders and educational change advocates ever since. For if teachers do not step forth and begin to lead change processes, can teaching ever truly become a profession? Without scaffolded opportunities for teachers to lead, are teachers forever doomed to fall back to the unholy trinity of conservatism, presentism, and privatism described in Chapter 1?

Our findings from the Mindful Teacher project are cautiously optimistic on this account. When Lortie wrote *Schoolteacher* in the 1970s and when Huberman conducted his studies in the 1980s, there was little momentum to foster teachers as researchers or as leaders. In the years since, there has been a sea change in education. Although efforts to develop teachers as researchers and leaders often are subject to the usual spasmodic, stop-and-go patterns endemic in educational change, we now are in a different era. School districts all over the nation have been supporting teachers' professional learning communities. Teachers are acquiring opportunities for differentiated roles such as literacy or math coaches in their buildings, and the revolution in information technology has enabled teachers to network with colleagues from across the country and indeed around the world on everything from effective teaching strategies for autistic children to multicultural education. An increasing amount of educational change is transnational in scope, enabling educators to learn not just from their colleagues down the hall or in a neighboring district, but also from other nations in locations as far removed as Finland, Japan, and Singapore.

In addition to these exciting new developments supporting teacher leadership in schools, scholars have documented that an older model of school leadership based upon a single charismatic principal does not fit our contemporary situation, for several reasons. The first of these is that although a few extraordinary individuals with strong leadership skills can be found from time to time, they are not available in large enough numbers in proportion to the number of schools in struggling circumstances (Hargreaves & Fink, 2006). Second, the sheer magnitude of a principal's job has ballooned so much in recent years that few educators are interested in becoming principals (Cusick, 2002; Hewitt, Pijanowski, Carnine, & Denny, 2008). This reality of "leadership in crisis" (Harris, 2008, p. 16) has created new pressures within schools to redistribute power and authority by viewing leadership not so much as the attribute of a single individual but rather as a network constituted by the interactions of administrators, teachers, and their situations (Spillane & Diamond, 2007). Third, a broader social evolution toward the "end of leadership" (Kellerman, 2012) as previously understood in the nonprofit and for-profit sectors is leading to a renewed interest in effective teamwork as the heart of thriving organizations.

The pressurized environment facing principals and the growth of distributed leadership are important, but these are not the only reasons for the growing interest in and practice of teacher leadership. Scholars have found that schools in which teachers provide more influential leadership are considered by the teachers themselves to be more effective, and student engagement is impacted significantly and positively by teacher leadership (Leithwood, Jantzi, & Steinbach, 1999). Fears that empowered teachers might lead to more adversarial relationships with administrators do not appear to be validated by the research, because that empowerment seems to accompany a rise in communicative competence within a school that increases teacher efficacy (Ingersoll, 2003). For most teachers, leadership is not expressed through random activities, but rather those that are focused on improving student learning (Murphy, Goldring, & Porter, 2006).

THREE LEVELS OF MINDFUL TEACHER LEADERSHIP

The vast majority of the teacher leadership that we documented and catalyzed through the Mindful Teacher seminars can be described as "micro-level" interventions. When Jeff made the book on El Salvador for Gregorio, when Grace worked patiently and steadfastly with Miguel to help him modify his behavior so that he could learn better, and when Karyn modified her classroom to contain Cecilia's "running," each teacher exemplified the experimentation that is at the heart of all good teaching. These were classroom-level changes that demonstrated the power of good teachers to assess the learning environment they had created among their students and to shift dimensions of their day-to-day instruction and interactions to support learning.

Yet mindful teacher participants also demonstrated "meso-level" leadership, especially in our seminar settings. One of the most striking findings from the seminars was that teachers continually discovered that a practice that they thought was districtwide turned out to be peculiar to the culture of their own buildings. Teachers helped one another to understand the role and power of school site councils, instructional leadership teams, and whole-school improvement plans. When violence spiked in the community, when a teacher strike was impending, or when mathematics and literacy coaches were cut due to a fiscal crisis, teachers continually were able to assist one another to learn what district policy was and what decisions appeared to have been made (sometimes without teacher involvement) in their buildings.

On the one hand, almost all of what we have come to call "mindful teacher leadership" happens at the micro-level. Teachers want their students to learn, and our focus each and every day isn't on adults, but on the children and young people who crowd our classrooms, eager to be engaged and to thrive. We know teachers also can benefit from meso-level activities like the Mindful Teacher seminars that allow us to share and spread knowledge within and across schools. But occasionally teachers have opportunities to move not only beyond their schools and their districts, but also beyond their states and even their nations. When teachers not only attend conferences but also present their work to one another and receive validation from others in professional settings, the result can be a powerful sense of catharsis and lateral learning. Teachers can then take what they have learned from these "macro-level" experiences back to their schools to inform their instructional practices and their teacher leadership in their districts. Just as is the case for all professionals, these opportunities to step outside of the classroom and garner new insights from others engaged in similar processes can be decisive catalysts for professional renewal and growth.

Liz MacDonald: Growing into Teacher Leadership

Back in the spring of 2005 when Dennis and I were writing our proposal for the Mindful Teacher project and envisioning what supports we may offer the teachers, I felt most adamant about including funding for teachers to attend professional conferences, which was an uncommon practice among most of the teachers I knew in the district. Due to the partnership work that I had done with Boston College, I was afforded the opportunity to not only attend but to present at several national conferences, including the American Educational Research Association, the National Council of Teachers of English, and the Holmes Partnership. Upon entering this previously unknown world of roundtable discussions, symposiums, and panel presentations, my educational knowledge was vastly expanded, yet I became even more alienated in my school building. How could I go back and tell my colleagues that I just spent three luxurious days in an exciting city listening to the most recent research, networking with educational leaders, and discussing the politics of school reform over a nice dinner with professors from schools of education?

I can vividly remember hearing an opening presentation about the No Child Left Behind Act at a conference in Washington, D.C., and then 6 months later attending a whole-school meeting in which the district had just begun to distribute literature about its implications for teaching and learning. On the one hand, I felt incredibly fortunate to have my professional life enriched. On the other hand, I was outraged that my colleagues at the ground level were not part of the conversations at these conferences.

In our third year of the Mindful Teacher project, the prospect of sharing our work with other teachers became a possibility when we learned about the upcoming International Conference on Teacher Research (ICTR) to be held at Bank Street College in New York City. The seminar teachers enthusiastically met up on a cold winter's night after a day of teaching to collectively write a proposal and send it off a day before the deadline.

After receiving a congratulatory acceptance letter from Cindy Ballenger, ICTR's program chair, the teachers' excitement mounted. What would we say? Who would be there? How would we travel?

Dennis then informed me that he would not be able to accompany us due to a prior personal commitment that weekend. Of course, I knew that this was his way of cutting the cord and allowing us all to exercise our professional expertise. What I did not realize at the time was how momentous this decision was and the tremendous impact it would have on the teachers, including myself.

The night before our presentation, we met up in the hotel lounge to finalize our presentation and make arrangements for the day. As the last member of our group of seven entered the lounge upon arrival into the city, we all cheered! We were hugging one another with an air of both anxiousness and exhilaration. "I can't believe we are actually here," we said to one another. "This is so cool!"

I myself was in awe of the fact that I was now the leader of this Mindful Teacher group, and they were looking to me for guidance about presenting at an international conference. The next morning, we took cabs over to the West Side on our journey to the conference. For most of us, this was going to be the first time both attending and presenting at a conference.

Once we arrived we listened to the keynote address by Vivian Gussin Paley. Entitled "Looking for Magpie: How to Locate Your Voice as Teacher and Researcher," Paley's words resonated with us, especially when she said that "the teacher is alone in the classroom looking for his or her voice." Here we were presenting about the Mindful Teacher, and we knew that sense of loneliness was such a big part of the alienated teaching that we all had experienced.

After breaking up to attend a variety of presentations during the first session, we met up for lunch, where teachers shared their excitement and nervousness about our upcoming symposium. I told the teachers not to be disappointed if our session was not well attended, reminding them that this was our first public engagement and we might not attract a large audience. At the same time, I tried to speak to everyone I met to encourage them to come to our presentation.

Contrary to my prediction, our session was jam-packed, with people still entering minutes after we began. Many of the audience had no space left to sit but on the floor! We had divided ourselves up so that each of us was able to share the origin, purpose, and themes of the Mindful Teacher. The energy from the crowd motivated the presenters, and I felt pride as I watched my colleagues take over with ease and confidence. Many lingered after the presentation, asking the participants questions, exchanging email addresses, and commenting on the need of such a group at their school or partnership school.

One of the highlights of the day came when Ann Lieberman, coauthor of a book on teacher leadership that we read for discussion at one of our Mindful Teacher seminars, came over to talk with us. I had previously met Ann at a conference in Chicago and discussed the project's work over breakfast, during which she offered some helpful advice about teacher leadership. More importantly, Ann validated and appreciated my own work as a teacher leader, giving me the assurance to continue my work. The teachers were blown away that Ann Lieberman was before them, chatting informally about the conference and their work as teacher researchers. At that moment I could truly feel their excitement and was happy to see them now part of the conversation. We ended the day with a celebratory dinner back on the East Side where we were staying, but the real revelry has manifested in a variety of ways since that day.

Presenting at the conference as a group of teachers without a university member present gave us all a great sense of agency along with an affirmation that what teachers think does matter. The group had an opportunity to interact with student teachers, teachers, administrators, professors, and researchers who were open-minded, caring, and able to slow down to think and reflect upon their practices and the current policies in education. Jeff later shared with me that he "wished we could take everyone from this conference and put them on an island and all teach together." The insular world of the teacher's classroom, school building, and district had been expanded to one in which each of us could express our thoughts and opinions without fearing any ramifications. We were able to recognize ourselves as teacher leaders who could share our experiences with colleagues not just from around the country but even around the globe.

We don't know if the teachers at the conference who shared their enthusiasm with us know just what an impact their support had on us. We returned home eager to carry on our work to another stage. We applied for and received another 3-year grant from the Boston Collaborative Fellows program to continue the Mindful Teacher seminars. This time, we stretched our work to include "superintendent schools." A superintendent school is one that is identified for special assistance in the district because of its low test-score results.

Although the idea was that the Mindful Teacher project would be helping struggling and underperforming schools, something else happened. I learned that my own school, as part of a districtwide cost-saving measure, was to be closed and consolidated into a nearby middle school, along with another neighborhood elementary school. Although we had known at my school that our enrollments were low and the economy seemed to be getting worse and worse by the minute, the news still was devastating. Over the summer, one of my colleagues had been chosen to be our new principal, and we had spent months planning how we were going to all collaborate and plan together to make the new year better than ever.

What to do? I took the issue to the Mindful Teacher seminar. It turns out that the participating teachers from superintendent schools, who had many more years in the district than I did, had lots of great advice for me and my colleagues about how to guide this process. They pointed out potential advantages with becoming part of a K–8 school and named all kinds of programs and services that we could tap into. They also encouraged us to speak up so that we wouldn't just be on the receiving end of bad news but could shape the environment in ways that would help our kids in the new building. With the help of my Mindful Teacher colleagues, I mustered the courage to speak before the Boston School Committee, urging committee members to let teachers be part of the whole transition process.

How did mindfulness enter into this? We knew that the Boston Public Schools were facing a financial crisis. We knew that our school's neighborhood of Allston-Brighton was undergoing rapid demographic change, and that the number of families with children had decreased. Superintendent Carol Johnson had to cut costs somewhere in light of the dire financial situation, and our school seemed like an obvious candidate.

Mindfulness entered in because our first impulse to attack the district leadership and defend our school really wouldn't help in light of the financial crisis. Superintendent Johnson had a tough job, and it wouldn't help anything to make it tougher. So our role was to ask for real inclusion and a real voice in the process. Our role was to make sure that our kids wouldn't get shortchanged, but would have a chance to thrive in a building that was first built and then set up for middle school kids.

Please, teacher friends and colleagues who are reading this book, don't think that we are saying that we have all of the answers! When I think back to some of my dark days of teaching prior to the Mindful Teacher project when I was on the verge of leaving the profession, feelings of alienation, failure, and unhappiness immediately resurface in my memory. Since that time, pacing guides, high-stakes accountability, and taxing students have not disappeared. There are still days that I teeter on despair and feel like giving up the fight to educate all children despite the external factors beyond my control.

It is at those times that I rely most heavily on one of the basic tenets of mindful teaching: stopping.

I stop to contemplate why I teach and am reminded, like many of you reading this now.

I teach because I care.

I care about all of the children and especially for those who require support, guidance, and stability both emotionally and academically and for whom school may be the only place they find it.

I care about the quality of education of urban school children who have too often had their standards lowered.

I care about the families who do not have the human or social capital to seek out the best resources for themselves and their children.

I care about my fellow educators who have fought long and hard for the rights of teachers and have weathered many a storm of reform. Some of them have done this for as many years as I have lived!

And I care about the profession of teaching and the future it holds for all of the young, bright, and fervent individuals who have the power to legitimize the importance of good teaching.

And then I reach out to those around me who care too.

REACHING OUT

We hope that you have acquired a number of tools in this chapter for thinking about how you might reach out to others if you are inspired to work mindfully as an educator. We hasten to reiterate a theme that has come up again and again in the foregoing pages: *For any of these tools to work, they have to be adapted wisely to your own situation.* To make this adaptation effective, you have to draw upon the full repertoire of your professional expertise, consulting your experience, the range of available data, and situational factors such as competing reforms, student demographic trends, and the impact of the current economic recession on resource allocation. Only if these tools are mediated by open-minded and caring educators who want to take their prior experiences and skills seriously and who see teaching as a *vocation* (from the Latin *vocare*, meaning "call," in the sense of a "calling") will the tools be able to realize the humanistic purposes for which they are intended.

To summarize some of our key points made throughout this chapter, we now review our *eightfold strategies, seven synergies,* and the *triple tensions* of mindful teaching. The strategies are presented here in the event that you would like to establish a similar seminar structure in your school or district, and the synergies are indicators you can adjust and modify as you reflect upon your teaching alone or with colleagues at the end of a busy day or over the weekend. Finally, the triple tensions are intended to remind you that you are operating in a dynamic context with many factors beyond your control that nonetheless may be subject to your skillful modulation and eventual transformation.

Our *eightfold strategies* for a seminar setting are as follows:

1. Create a safe and trusting climate for sharing teachers' **pressing concerns**, as soon as possible after teachers arrive in the seminar setting.
2. Encourage openness through **selective vulnerability** by choosing in advance a topic of individual concern identified by a teacher leader that others can relate to based on similar experiences with their own students or colleagues.
3. Bring **scholarly research** to bear on a given topic through careful study and preparation outside of the seminar setting.
4. Practice **formal meditation**, both in the seminar setting and at home, to calm and focus the mind and to be open and attuned to new information.
5. Enable small-group work on the **psychological intrusions** that arise during formal meditation to bring forth the range of concerns preoccupying seminar participants.
6. Use a **tuning protocol** to go deeper on an issue of special importance to an individual, especially when the topic is time-sensitive and the individual would appreciate concentrated attention as soon as possible.
7. Enable **extended debriefing** on both the tuning protocol and the entire session, including time to discuss readings and activities for the next seminar.
8. Establish **mindfulness assignments** that assist teachers to focus on the many domains of instruction and learning that easily

can escape our awareness in the demanding press of events in our schools.

This structure is in turn supported by the following *seven synergies* of mindful teaching:

1. **Open-mindedness**, or "detachment from views," so that teachers practice seeing the validity of multiple perspectives on complicated issues related to curriculum choices or administrators' and policymakers' decisions
2. A **caring and loving** disposition, so that teachers do not neglect the spiritual and emotional dimension of their vocation
3. **Stopping**—either through formal meditation or informal reflection, so that teachers mitigate *reactivity* in favor of more considered *responsiveness*
4. **Professional expertise**—respect for the entire ensemble of knowledge required of teachers today, spanning from the design and implementation of differentiated instruction to communication with parents to diverse modalities of studying and drawing inferences from pupil achievement data
5. **Authentic alignment**, so that teachers make sure that their convictions and their practices are harmonized with one another, and experienced as such by their students
6. **Integration**, so that all pedagogical repertoires and choices are exploited and related to one another in the best interests of the students
7. **Collective responsibility**, so that teachers work on an ongoing basis with all social sectors to share appropriately in the education of the young

To achieve their optimal efficacy, these seven synergies must be interdependent. None is complete without a relationship of dynamic equilibrium with each of the other coordinates. One can't intend to be *loving* and yet neglect one's *professional expertise* as an educator. One can't claim to be *open-minded* and yet fail to *stop* and consider what a student might mean when offering an unusual interpretation of a short story.

Finally, the *triple tensions* of mindful teaching point to permanent dilemmas of teaching and learning that cannot ever be completely overcome, except during the briefest of moments. In many ways, *they define the instructional situation.* These are the tensions between the following aspects of teaching:

1. **Contemplation and action**, because one can always need more time to think, just as one can always respond impulsively, but the real art of mindful teaching needs a carefully attuned integration of theory and practice
2. **Ethics and power**, because a preoccupation with ethics can lead one to withdraw from the public sphere, and an excessive concern with power leads invariably to corruption and narcissism
3. The **individual and the collective**, because on some occasions a courageous individual is needed to speak truth to power, but in other instances individuals need to subordinate their own wishes to those of the majority out of respect for democratic processes and values

As a teacher, you enter into dynamic relationships with your students from the moment they enter your room. A different climate exists at the beginning of a given class than exists in the middle or at the end. It is your challenge to create a classroom environment that modulates the contradictions manifested in the triple tensions in a way that best serves your students, even as you remain mindful that there are many factors in a given room that you have not freely chosen but that you have been assigned with varying degrees of assent and coercion. Bringing the seven synergies to bear on the triple tensions so that they promote deep learning is one of your major tasks.

In addition to the eightfold structure, the seven synergies, and the triple tensions, readers are invited to consider three levels of mindful teacher leadership. At the *micro-level,* you are already constantly revising and reflecting upon your educational interactions with children and young people. *This* is where your energies should be focused, and if at any point mindful teacher leadership distracts you from this core commitment, you must return to that axial relationship without which all else fails.

At the *meso-level,* teacher groups that meet within and across schools invite opportunities for honing one's professional expertise. The Mindful Teacher seminars provided us with one free and independent setting for creating such a teacher network. Almost every district is characterized by a multitude of initiatives in this regard.

Our central question for such initiatives inquires about the degree of teacher ownership in launching or steering a network. At this given historical moment, teachers are especially needful of opportunities to bring forth their own ideas and to lead their own initiatives, with sympathetic yet also occasionally challenging outsiders as strategic allies.

Finally, although we agree with the numerous findings on teacher leadership that warn against reforms that take teachers too far away from their students, we also know that any situation where professors, administrators, and philanthropists regularly have opportunities to network at educational conferences, but teachers do not, cannot lead to the kinds of educational improvement we need today. We can't have jet-setting school-change *surfers* and classroom-bound teacher *serfs*!

Teachers need forums like the ICTR to share their professional growth as well as their challenges with one another. These forums or conferences provide venues for exploring and advocating *macro-level* changes. Just as professors find validation outside of their universities by presenting their ideas and research to colleagues from other higher education institutions, so do teachers need such opportunities for professional renewal and growth. These opportunities need to entail not just listening and taking in information, but also submitting one's own ideas to the test in the court of professional opinion.

MINDFUL TEACHER LEADERSHIP IN ACTION

Although conferences provide important venues for sharing ideas and proven practices, ultimately we need to address the prosaic, everyday interactions of our lives in schools. We need greater continuity and sustainability in change processes than annual conferences can provide. We need to change our ongoing organizational cultures in schools.

The best work of which we are aware that is being undertaken in this regard at this point in time is that provided by the Arizona K12 Center in Phoenix (www.azk12.org). The Center is a nonprofit organization that enables educators to come together on a regular basis. The Center sponsors a Teacher Solutions Team that channels teacher-generated ideas and practices into the schools. We have worked with the Center for many years now and have been honored by the manner in which educators have embraced "mindful teacher leadership" and extended it into their own reflections and practices. In this way, the concept has taken on a life of its own in a setting far removed from our work in Boston.

Tara Dale, who teaches science at Akimel A-al Middle School, provides one example of mindful teacher leadership in action. She has worked with the Arizona Education Foundation, the Arizona K12 Center, the Rodel Foundation of Arizona, and the Arizona Education Association to create "Take Your Legislator to School Day." Tara knows that in a diverse multicultural democracy, one cannot expect policymakers to know everything about the needs of their diverse constituents. If one wants policymakers to understand a profession as challenging as that of education, one has to engage policymakers directly and proactively, for example, by inviting them to one's school. "I have two hopes," she writes. "One is that more legislators go into classrooms, and that this becomes the 'cool thing' to do as a legislator. The other hope is to take it to the next level, where a bill comes up and before they make a decision, they call and ask teachers what we think."

Mindful teaching and mindful teacher leadership are philosophical concepts. An innovation such as "Take Your Legislator to School Day" is just one illustration of how educators can reclaim their profession. For such ideas to endure, they need to be integrated into professional practices and networks.

Part of the way this has occurred through the Arizona K12 Center is by linking mindful teaching and mindful teacher leadership to the National Board for Professional Teaching Standards (www.nbpts .org). The National Board's standards and their affiliated five core propositions uphold the holistic development of students and teachers, with ongoing reflection and adaptation of curriculum and pedagogies as essential components of the profession. The Arizona K12 Center also hosts a website entitled "Stories from School" (www .storiesfromschoolaz.org). This provides teachers a venue for offering their own perspectives about the on-the-ground challenges of teachers and students today.

Teachers are at a tipping point in American education. Over half a million teachers leave the profession each year in the United States, costing the country $2.2 billion annually (Alliance for Excellent Education, 2014). Close to half of those leave within their first 5 years, before they have even reached the level of truly accomplished practice. This problem is especially acute in schools in struggling circumstances that serve low-income students of color. Teachers shouldn't just complain, but they do need to express their concerns as part of mindful teacher leadership. If they are to do this in a way that inspires hope and confidence in their students and among the public, they need to tap into the deepest wellsprings of their vocation.

TEACHING AS A SPIRITUAL PRACTICE

In his 1826 lectures at the University of Berlin, Friedrich Schleiermacher (2000, p. 13) defended what he referred to as "the dignity of pedagogy" in transmitting the cultural heritage of humanity to a rising generation. For Schleiermacher, teaching was a spiritual act, requiring exquisite attention to the choice of instructional approaches, the selection of curricula, and one's attunement to the developing child's interests and needs. Always culturally conditioned, it was the responsibility of educators to develop their intellectual capabilities to their fullest, continually alert to the reality that their instruction would have impacts upon the young that extended far beyond their completion of finite tasks.

In the decades following Schleiermacher's lectures, American reformers began adapting Germanic innovations to our own different circumstances, with everything from the kindergarten to the graded school to teacher training institutes and the research university very much derived from German antecedents. American thinkers such as the Transcendentalists (whose name derived from Immanuel Kant's "transcendental philosophy") promoted the rights of individuals to pursue their own life paths beyond the boundaries of prevailing social norms. Civil rights activist and educator W.E.B. DuBois, who studied at the University of Berlin, internalized the canon of German idealist philosophy and was a fierce, uncompromising advocate of the liberal arts. So did progressive educator John Dewey, who extended and modulated this heritage into his pragmatist philosophy on this side of the Atlantic.

Yet while this embrace of a broadly humanistic philosophy of education swept through many parts of American society, other tendencies were under way. The "feminization" of education in the United States—meaning the rise of a predominantly female teaching force in schools—was conjoined with a predominantly male research presence in universities (Lagemann, 2002). Adapting experimental research designs from the natural sciences and applying them to schools, researchers began a century-long objectification of teachers (Labaree, 2004). Although research has contributed to the improvement of education, power differentials between professors and teachers have endured and troubled the profession. As teachers have become inundated by wave after wave of reform, their own opportunities to define the profession have been thwarted. Teaching as a kind of spiritual practice, along lines articulated by Schleiermacher, has been marginalized in contemporary American education.

Yet just when one might consider contemporary trends to be irreversible, countervailing tendencies have emerged. Climate change and income inequality have prompted an exploration of the moral judgments that led policymakers and the public to ignore early warnings of impending danger (Pope Francis, 2015; Soros, 2008). The intellectual skills of the most talented mainstream economists have been exposed as inadequate when it came to the anticipation of the recent recession, not so much through a lack of technical expertise as through a failure of imagination (Piketty, 2014; Taleb, 2007). Increasingly, the wisest change advocates (Fullan, 2008; Sisodia, Wolfe, & Sheth, 2007) understand that the full range of human intelligence and not just "reactive problem solving" (Senge, Smith, Kruschwitz, Laur, & Schley, 2008, p. 50) will be needed to meet the challenges that lie ahead.

For some (Horn & Staker, 2015; Wagner & Dintersmith, 2015), the emergence of new digital technologies provides a promising venue for overcoming the strictures of recent accountability and testing regimes. This potential, however, can easily be distorted. In order to optimize the resources of new technologies and to minimize their problems, further inquiry is necessary.

CHAPTER 6

The Mindful Teacher
and Technology

Is there a special way that educators curious about mindful teaching should respond to the enormous changes in technology that have swept through our lives in the past decades? Critics (Jenkins, Clinton, Purushotma, Robison, & Weigel, 2006; Trilling & Fadel, 2009) have been largely accurate when they claim that educators on the whole have been resistant to new technologies in the public schools. This resistance must entail some deeper meaning about how educators experience their work and the opportunities and limitations of new technologies. Why have educators been skeptical towards boosters of technology in schools in some cases and almost viscerally opposed in others?

As always, proposed new reforms—whether they are related to site-based decision making, multiculturalism, or inquiry-based approaches—must pass through the powerful mediating fulcrum of teachers' workplace cultures. Teachers acquire these cultures through years of professional socialization. First, there are teachers' own experiences as pupils as they observed their teachers from the perspective of those receiving instruction and attempting to master content knowledge. Second, there is another level of socialization as teacher candidates in colleges and universities learn about dimensions of the profession such as lesson planning, classroom management, and assessment practices. Third, there is the actual immersion into the workplace setting of the classroom that often is determinative in regard to shaping teachers' daily experiences.

This triple ensemble of enculturation—as students, as teacher candidates, and as practicing teachers—powerfully shapes how teachers develop their professional norms and ethics; technical skills related to planning, introducing, guiding, and assessing instruction; and soft skills involved in encouraging struggling learners. They lead teachers to accept an egalitarian culture that promotes noninterference in one another's classrooms. They create a wary attitude toward outsiders who promulgate innovations without due consideration to the additional work such innovations entail for teachers. This is especially the case when innovators give little evidence of understanding the skills that teachers must martial to manage the bustle and intensity of instructing large groups of young people day in and day out over many years.

Teachers' jobs are demanding; however, this does not mean that one can completely opt out of the digital revolution. Given the range of technological possibilities opened up in recent years, how can educators adjudicate which approaches to take to its integration in the years ahead? Educators need to draw upon their philosophies of education, new research findings, and their accumulated professional repertoires to mediate new technologies. To do so requires educators to take the time to work out their core values in communities of inquiry that are open to novelty and debate. These communities must encourage respect for dissidents and promote lifelong learning that is not just measurable but also ambiguous and unsettling. With such a philosophical compass to adjudicate and filter emerging social trends, educators can both consolidate their professional convictions and support purposeful growth through the assimilation of new information.

THE SEVEN SYNERGIES AS A COMPASS

The seven synergies of mindful teaching outlined in the previous chapter provide such a compass that educators can use both to appropriate the positive aspects of new technologies and to deflect their negative facets. In many ways, the seven synergies bear affinities to Wolfgang Klafki's (1994, 2000) questions of "didactic analysis" that he argued all educators must address in their lesson planning. Klafki wanted educators to ask what horizons a given curriculum would open to children's curiosity and imagination, and he demanded that educators ask not just what a curriculum meant in terms of children's future occupational prospects but also what the curriculum could mean for children today. Although now is not the time for an in-depth comparison of the seven synergies of mindful teaching with Klafki's didactic analysis, one should note that both frameworks place ethics explicitly at the center of teaching as a vocation.

Given this ethical lens, how might we use the seven synergies to help us adjudicate the proper use of technology that could move

beyond the problematic dimensions that have become evident in previous reforms? Is it possible to imagine that we can buffer the stop–
start, push–pull pressures of outside interest groups, including those
of for-profit computer corporations? Can we temper the hyperbole of
technology advocates on the one hand and move beyond the hostility
of those who have become close-minded to the potential of technology on the other? What can the idea of mindful teaching and learning
contribute to these questions? Let us investigate, and in the process,
see if we can imagine a future in which technology contributes to
mindful teaching and learning.

First Synergy: Open-Mindedness. In almost no other facet of
contemporary society have generational divides become so palpably
manifest as in the use of technology (Rosen, 2011). The fault lines
are clear. Baby boomers, born between 1946 and 1964, and members of Generation X, born between 1965 and 1979, have appreciated new technologies but tend to use them instrumentally rather
than as ends in themselves. For subsequent generations—such as
Generation Y, born in the remaining years of the 20th century, and
the iGeneration, born in the new millennium—technology access
and use is easy and omnipresent.

It has become a truism to refer to Generation Y and the iGeneration as "digital natives" (Palfrey & Gasser, 2008) who have learned
how to access, manipulate, and produce their own content in new
technologies. Enormous numbers of young people, in emerging as well
as advanced economies, have not only consumed material they have
accessed on the web through iTunes or Facebook, but have produced
their own web-based materials through mashups, the creation and
embellishment of avatars, and participation in multiuser shared habi-
tats (Ito, 2010; Montgomery, 2007). Teenagers in the United States are
now sending more than 3,000 text-messages a month, and depending
on the number of their friends, can easily be receiving double that
number in return (Nielsen Company, 2010). They have developed
their own skillful deployment of emoticons and abbreviations, such as
"cu" for "see you." They abandon older providers—such as Myspace
and Facebook—when those providers fail to meet their needs; they
subsequently endorse ever-more efficient and engaging apps based on
their ease of use and adaptability.

There are so many opportunities for play and creativity in new
technology forums that older forms of curriculum and instruction

can seem downright cruel in comparison. If one makes an error on a computer game or setting up photographs on a Facebook page, for example, one usually can correct it quickly and then move on to another activity; this is quite different than on a standardized test where the results are fixed in space and time. Classroom interactions can be excruciating for children who stutter or are autistic; conversely, online gamers can pause as long as they like without loss of cache. In the world of online interaction, breaks in time are usual and expected. For children who are talented in the layout of visual designs but clumsy with words, opportunities to show what they can do when adding maps to history projects or artwork to an English essay can provide welcome relief and the opportunity to showcase their strengths rather than reluctantly reveal their weaknesses.

Second Synergy: Caring and Loving. Mindful teaching should recognize not just the rights of dominant groups but also the needs of diverse learners. Attentiveness to the selection of new technological tools—and their ramifications for young people—must proceed with full recognition of the educational import of these decisions. *All* educators bear a common responsibility if they fail to communicate to young people the indelible digital footprint that they leave behind when they neglect to apply strict privacy settings on their accounts, send messages to friends in which they expose themselves, or leave messages or photographs on blogs or on Flicker that will damage their reputations for years to come. If we care about our young people, we will make sure that they learn about online predators and identity theft, and that they also learn that the Internet contains dimensions that can be mercilessly cruel to the unguarded and the vulnerable.

Enthusiasm for technology and its wonders must also proceed with a discussion of appropriate calibration of technology in our lives. With technology so omnipresent, what is lost in terms of quiet time in nature, focused attention on the brush strokes of an artist, the sonorous bow of a cello, or face-to-face communication between individuals? And when the young do put down their cellphones or turn off their laptops, are there adults in their lives who are fully present and available to them, or are the adults themselves modeling sedentary lives of distraction and consumption?

The incorporation of technology must proceed *respectfully* for the good of both teachers and students—without forced mandates and without the frequent condescension allocated to educators who question the value of technological change or whose first experiences have led to failed lessons when a software program freezes up, a Skype connection breaks off, or a sound system is distorted. Subtleties in the shift of classroom dynamics that technology creates must be investigated. For example, if students are practicing memorizing the conjugation of irregular verbs in a foreign language, does their practice on individual iPhones advance the learning of some students but retard the development of others who need a more collective exercise? How can we let our students know that as educators, their well-being must always be our top priority, and that we care about them not just as test-score producers on the one hand or gamers on the other, but as learners rich in their own unique singular identities and hitherto unrealized human potential?

Third Synergy: Stopping. Technology has given us everything from the complete works of Shakespeare and the exact topography of South Africa to dozens of archived films of the Chilean New Song Movement and interviews with winners of Olympic games of years past. Educators who know how to access these materials, and who can guide young people to embed them in artfully designed classroom presentations, now have a world of resources at their fingertips. Advocates (Gee, 2007; Jenkins et al., 2006; Trilling & Fadel, 2009) of technology rightfully want to help educators capitalize on these materials, believing that the technology itself will engage young people turned off by the bureaucracy and boredom of schools as they now exist.

The impatience of technology advocates for rapid transformation in education is understandable—but also often one-sided and without due recognition of the problems that come along with new technologies. We have an abundance of data to indicate that the sheer number of hours youth are spending in front of their handheld devices, iPads, and desktops is correlated with all sorts of negative outcomes, including everything from depression to the inability to adapt to delayed gratification to an underdeveloped ability to empathize with others in real time (Small & Vorgan, 2009). Sherry Turkle (2011, 2015) has argued that even though young people may have hundreds of online friends, few of these friends are available in the event of a real-life crisis. Teachers find themselves competing with social networks for students' attention—and losing. Nicholas Carr (2010) contends that the Internet is actually making us stupid, especially because of its advocates who claim that knowing information is irrelevant in our new world.

For evidence that Carr is on to something important, consider *Most Likely to Succeed: Preparing Our Kids for the Innovation Era* (2015) by Tony Wagner and Ted Dintersmith. The authors find it absurd to ask students to spend time memorizing "the placement of accent marks in French vocabulary," "the definition of an isosceles triangle," and "the definition of covalent bonds" (pp. 143–144). The argument is that "content knowledge is no longer valued in the workplace" (p. 27).

The prospect that the cosmopolitan citizens of the future might do well by committing to memory the details of a foreign language, the intricacies of geometry, or the beauty of chemistry is lost in such best-selling books. The authors do not question the dangers of excessive dependency on Google, with its algorithms based on popularity rather than evidence, as a fountain of wisdom. Is there nothing worth learning thoroughly beyond what currently is privileged by the fleeting vagaries of the market? Wise parents, and conscientious teachers, will consider it their responsibility that students are enabled to learn a curriculum thoroughly, which will mean learning some of it by heart.

Schools cannot make it their task to identify all potential problems that arise with Internet use. The problems are too labyrinthine. But schools can espouse philosophies of education that promote the self-regulation of the young. They can help young people recognize the pleasures that are to be found by slowing time down to attend to the subtleties of a sunset, the nuance in a jazz improvisation, and the modulation in an opera singer's interpretation of an aria. It may be, given the accelerated pace of life today, that an explicit curriculum in stopping, observing, and reflecting should be designed. Such a curriculum could expose young people to research on the dangers of excessive Internet use and the need to balance time online with an active social life offline, as well as time for physical exercise and the pleasure of solitude in nature. With such a curriculum, educators can encourage students to explore ways of being in the world that need not be technologically mediated, such as a quiet conversation with a friend (Turkle, 2015). Educators could help students to move beyond *surfing* and *browsing* to promote *stopping* and *thinking*.

Fourth Synergy: Professional Expertise. Ralph Tyler (1949), in *Basic Principles of Curriculum and Instruction*, described a reactive response to whatever the trends of the present day might be as a "cult of 'presentism'" (p. 18). In this classic text of curriculum theory, Tyler contended that a better approach was to filter contemporary pressures through two lenses. The first of these concerned educators' philosophical commitments. What values do educators stand for? The second of these concerned research about learning. What do we know about the ways that students understand the world?

Tyler's stance, in many ways, bears similarities with the *Didaktik* tradition of continental Europe (Hopmann, 2007) and especially with Klafki's (1958/2000, 1994) articulation of guiding questions to use in filtering curricular materials. In this understanding, educators have a professional obligation to be clear about their ethics, to inquire into the present meaning and future implications of curricular choices, and to keep abreast of current research findings. Without these, one is simply reacting to the winds of fashion.

After John Dewey, Tyler is arguably the most important U.S. curriculum theorist of the 21st century. *Basic Principles of Curriculum and Instruction* has been translated into many languages and has been used for planning purposes in dozens of systems around the world. It is important to note, however, that Tyler later amended some of his positions. A quarter of a century later, Tyler wrote,

> I would give much greater emphasis now to careful consideration of the implications for curriculum development of the active role of the student in the learning process. I would also give much greater emphasis to a comprehensive examination of the nonschool areas of student learning in developing curriculum. (Tyler, 1977/1993, p. 395)

In regard to the latter, Tyler explicitly mentioned the power of new technologies:

> Since the viewing of television represents for young people the major use of their waking hours, the development of knowledge, skills, attitudes, interests, and habits that will increase the value of this activity is very important. (Tyler, 1977/1993, pp. 399–400)

Perhaps because of reformers' advocacy regarding the potential value of television as an instructional tool, the floodgates were opened for too many teachers to inundate their classrooms with excerpts from game shows, soap operas, and sporting events that have entertainment value but are of limited merit when attempting to prepare youth to enter a world full of social injustice, economic breakdowns, and environmental catastrophes. Yet, we have to recall that Tyler never relented on the need for educators to filter curricular content through their philosophies and through research findings. To the degree that he evaded articulating a philosophy of education—and set about showing how to implement a curriculum regardless of one's philosophy—it may be that he inadvertently contributed to an evasion of moral values that has left educators adrift when confronted with complex curricular decisions. But this deficit does not mean that subsequent educators cannot reconstruct curriculum theory to provide precisely that missing philosophical foundation.

It is here that the concept of mindful teaching may be of service. Mindful teaching aspires to be ethical in principle and practice at once. Every action—the way a class is begun, how activities are planned and the moderated, which students are given opportunities to speak and which are marginalized—and all of these dimensions are viewed as saturated with meaning-making and requiring continuous reflection. Creating the enabling conditions for mindful teaching to occur, and devoting meticulous attention to our students' learning, can ensure that professional expertise is anchored in moral leadership.

Fifth Synergy: Authentic Alignment. The concept of *authentic alignment* was proposed as a way to gauge whether the diverse components of a professional field—its practitioners, its domain of knowledge and skills, and its field or institutions—enable individuals to do their very best to support the public good. In Charles Payne's analysis (2008) of urban school cultures in the United States, virtually any innovation is rapidly sabotaged by teachers who have developed a dogged mistrust of outsiders who seem to come and leave their schools with all of the predictability of a change of seasons. Even when the teachers have aligned their practices with official prescriptions, the new pedagogy isn't really given a chance to take hold. This is because it is implemented too often in name only, without an accompanying inner adjustment to its requirements.

Payne cautions reformers to attend to the *processes* of change before rushing to anticipated *outcomes*. Schools are complicated institutions, and school cultures reflect deep social divisions that fall out along lines of race, class, and immigrant status. Blindness to the complexity of these unresolved social issues, amplified by broader social problems much larger than schools themselves, only reinforces the gravity of the problems as dynamics of mistrust and negativity go unaddressed and are compounded over time.

Is technology infused into schools through ongoing dialogue with students and teachers, or is it simply installed as part of administrative fiat? Is technology the top priority for expenditures in a school or district when teacher positions are being cut and a crime wave sweeps through a struggling community? Educators need to know that reformers understand the on-the-ground realities of their lives, including the precariousness of support and the ways in which they occasionally find themselves on the defensive. Authentic alignment is difficult to attain even in the most favorable of circumstances, because there are so many variables shaping the lives of professionals, the domain of technical expertise is evolving, and the field of the institutions is unfolding. Yet, because the quest for authentic alignment by professionals is so great—because our longing for meaning and purpose in our work is so deeply human—the aspiration for its realization is never-ending. Understanding that the aspiration precedes and transcends technology in schools, thus, is a precondition for its humanistic incorporation into education. Technology, properly calibrated, becomes a means for the realization of potential—not the end in itself.

Sixth Synergy: Integration. Integrating networks have been advocated as a "catalyst of cohesion" (Hargreaves & Shirley, 2009b, pp. 99–101) that can help the components of a new change architecture to be mutually supportive rather than disconnected. New technologies are rich in potential for supporting integrating networks and for helping individuals to move their practice beyond the level of iconoclastic pioneer to a more collective practice. If authentic alignment is not so much an individual experience as a collective process of meaning-making and knowledge sharing, then integration is a necessary complement to the fifth synergy.

Not all networks are technologically mediated, even in the new millennium. Large-scale school reform strategies can indeed be effective, provided that there is an agile, precise, and sustainable set of practices that teachers can create and spread from one school to another through site visits, regional workshops, and national or provincial meetings. In England, networks called *performance federations* that link strong schools with struggling schools have been shown to be effective in lifting achievement in the latter schools without damaging it in the former (Chapman & Muijs, 2013). In rural Mexican middle schools, *comunidades de aprendizaje*, or *learning communities*, of professionals across schools likewise have improved student learning (Rincón-Gallardo, 2015).

The haphazard nature of technology adoption to promote integration—surging in one district, neglected in another, and erratic in a third—indicates a topic to be explored in greater depth. Fine new empirical work (Daly, 2010), supplemented by sophisticated conceptual advancements, is now exploring the power of social networks to enact change. Technology is especially promising in regard to integration because its ability to enhance sociability and access to information is so powerful. In the Northwest Rural Innovation and Student Engagement (RISE) program with which one of us is now working, technology platforms are helping remote rural educators to collaborate in lesson planning in ways they never could have done before (O'Connor, forthcoming). In this case, technology use is twinned with biannual meetings of educators from small towns to build professional learning communities they have never experienced before. It is in the interaction between technological innovations and other forms of real-life exchange that sustainable leadership occurs (Hargreaves & Fink, 2006).

Seventh Synergy: Collective Responsibility. Adults can easily express exasperation with the young for their fixation on and perhaps even addiction to new technologies, but then, as adults, we need to ask ourselves: What social spaces do we provide the young to interact with expansive and dynamic social networks outside of the compulsory environment of school? Employees in stores and shopping malls often distrust the young, and there is no purposeful role to play or activity for the young to accomplish in many informal social settings. Home environments too often do not provide testing grounds for developing one's autonomy or challenging one's limits. Adults in too many settings model for their children distracted, rushed lives that leave little time for quiet introspection or unhurried conversation (Turkle, 2015).

The seventh synergy of *collective responsibility* is taken from the Finnish model of blending achievement with equity (Sahlberg, 2015). Collective responsibility, in this cultural understanding, does not place the full onus for learning on schools. There is a recognition that many factors—a child's home life, his or her parents' income level, and access to museums and concerts, for example—play decisive roles in the education of the young.

Recent federal policies have focused on holding schools accountable with little acknowledgment of the roles of poverty and social disorganization in hindering learning. In the absence of adult commitment to being fully present with the young, it should cause little wonder that young people find themselves convening with such regularity in the new technologically mediated spaces of the Internet. The very architecture of our cities and suburbs is often organized without attention given to the needs of the young to have their own places to congregate.

Adults have defaulted on our collective responsibility for the young in this regard. We need to expand our offerings to young people to prove themselves through team-building exercises in the wilderness, performing and visual arts offerings in our cities, or traditional art forms such as calligraphy or dance that allow them to explore dimensions of self-discovery other than those mediated by the computer screen. UNESCO (2013) data reveal that the United States has fallen behind other industrialized nations by failing to develop effective policies for reducing our high rates of out-of-wedlock births, school dropout, childhood poverty, and childhood obesity. Although individuals have some measure of responsibility for these phenomena, everyone is implicated in them. We all share a collective responsibility for child well-being.

A TOOL, NOT A TALISMAN

The seven synergies are not just useful to educators in judging their aspirations for mindful teaching. They also can be used as indicators to assess how we are utilizing new technologies in schools. The indicators should be used to open up conversations and never to foreclose them. Although some research points to dangerous outcomes of new technologies in regard to distraction, depression, and sleeplessness, in many cases there are opposing points of view that reveal flaws in research designs or a rush to judgment. Discussions with the young themselves reveal a plurality of opinions on the strengths and limitations of new technologies. This is an arena that has so many facets that the imperative to stay open-minded and not to foreclose any vantage point will be especially important in the years to come. We are dealing with trade-offs in many cases. Wisdom requires attentiveness and compassion, especially for the young who have come to depend on new technologies as part of their identities.

Is technology being promoted as a panacea that will leave students who crave eye contact and express themselves well through gestures and movement at the margins of our classrooms? Can technology help students to understand the challenges faced by young people struggling with poverty or AIDS in other part of the world? Is there an upper limit to how much time we want our young people to spend in front of computer screens or using cellphones, and how do we offer to them a broad repertoire of learning experiences in which computers play little or no part? These larger ethical issues belong at the center of education and must not become marginalized or added in to reform plans after all of the measurable targets have been identified.

Technology cannot address all of the problems of alienated teaching, but it can connect educators with one another and with valuable resources for enriching lessons and improving assessment. Technology refers to the study and use of tools. This can be done in a mindful and measured manner. When implemented in this manner, technology may help to modify and alleviate the problems our schools are experiencing today. It may introduce play, creativity, and innovation into formal education in ways that were impossible just 10 or 15 years ago.

CHAPTER 7

Changing Whole Schools Mindfully

What would need to happen for mindful teaching to be a collective, rather than an individual, enterprise? Can we imagine ways in which not just isolated teachers, but whole schools and their school systems experience and promote mindful teaching? What would have to occur for such a transformation to take place?

We can learn much from those who are leading the quiet revolution of mindfulness education. More and more schools are incorporating contemplative practices into their schedules. Mindful Schools is the world's leading nonprofit on contemplative practices in education (www.mindfulschools.org). Mindful Schools has trained over 300,000 students in meditation and is at the vanguard of this movement. There are also now thousands of schools in which yoga is a regular physical education offering (www.yogainschools.corg). The quiet revolution in which students and teachers have opportunities to stop and are invited to experience life more fully is under way.

Room to Breathe (www.roomtobreathefilm.com) is a beautiful film on how mindfulness meditation helped to calm restless youngsters in a middle school in Oakland, California, that had suffered the highest suspension rates in the district. It is essential viewing for educators. *Healthy Habits of Mind* (www.mindfulschools.org/resources/healthy-habits-of-mind/), also promoted by Mindful Schools, is a documentary that blends classroom footage with brain research on the benefits of contemplative practices.

We view the work of Mindful Schools and other supports for teachers, such as Parker Palmer's professional development offerings (www.courageandrenewal.org), as necessary complements to the work that we conducted in the Mindful Teacher seminars. Such resources provide openings for the transformation of schools into places of learning and joy. They introduce new vocabularies and ways of relating into schools that can rectify the imbalances caused by data-driven decision making. At the same time, stand-alone professional development offerings often lack necessary street-level credibility to be well received by those who work in urban schools.

To skeptics, mindfulness can seem naive. It can become a caricature: the dying gasp of the Woodstock generation. Some advocates of mindfulness in education can seem uninformed about the school sanctions put in place by policymakers and the impacts of poverty on the lives of the young. Others are not aware of just how many external initiatives are brought into schools, the demands that these place upon teachers, and how fleeting many new projects turn out to be.

Ultimately, you can't be an outsider to the profession if you want to improve education. You have to become a part of the system and the school culture that you seek to change. That requires more than occasional professional development, and it takes more than goodwill. It takes years of steadfast dedication focused on the heart of the enterprise: teaching and learning. It takes years of hard-won trust among educators who work in the most challenging circumstances because that is where they are needed most. Those educators know well the difference between the effervescent enthusiasm of outside interlopers and the integrity of those who are in the schools day after day, week after week, and year after year.

Liz MacDonald: The Power of Mindful School Leadership

After 14 years as a classroom teacher in the BPS, the Garfield Elementary School where I had been teaching for most of my career was closing. We were merging with a nearby middle school as part of the district's effort to create more K–8 schools. At this juncture I decided to leave the classroom.

My next move was to accept a previously offered position as a literacy coach so that I could gain a better overview of what was happening in the BPS as a system. I knew that I would miss having my own classroom, but I was excited by the new opportunity. I would be working for an academic superintendent who oversaw over 30 schools in the district. I would be working with principals and teachers to support literacy practices in their schools and collaborating with the literacy department to create curriculum.

I would deliver professional development and analyze data with district-level leaders to identify trends of growth and need within and among schools.

In my first few months as a coach, I was driving around town from school to school to meet with principals, facilitate grade-level team meetings, and deliver professional development. As a result, I gained a greater appreciation of how demanding the principals' jobs were and how isolated they often felt from one another. This gave me a whole new awareness of how diverse the system was and how many strengths and challenges there were out there. Garfield had been on the western edge of the city, close to the suburbs. As I began working in more inner-city environments, I came to appreciate that Garfield actually had been relatively fortunate in its access to resources, including the Lynch School of Education at Boston College.

I discovered stark differences among the schools in the BPS. Some schools were places where stocked and organized book-rooms existed, and innovative practices such as guided reading had been implemented for years. Other schools had no updated collections of books, and professional development had been limited to operational or logistical matters of the school. There were schools whose populations consisted of more than 20% special education students or over 50% students learning a second language, both requiring additional and specialized supports. Other schools' percentages could be as low as 3%, demanding less resources.

There were huge differences in schools' cultures and in the ways that teachers organized their work. In some schools, teachers had opportunities to work collaboratively during identified grade-level team time or during instructional leadership team meetings. I loved working in these schools, where I felt I was a true professional working with colleagues who had the best interests of all of the children in their buildings at heart.

But then there were schools where teachers worked in silos. It seemed that in some of these schools the teachers had no experience of what it meant to work in a professional learning community. Academic freedom was the priority. This was nice for individual teachers who put a priority on their individual freedom. But the teachers didn't know what their colleagues were doing. I could see that as a result, the children's learning suffered.

And then there were differences in the infrastructure. Some schools were massive concrete buildings whose upkeep and general maintenance had been minimal. This was reflected in the smell of urine in the hallways and the dilapidated classroom spaces.

Across town, in another building, I would find shiny floors and flowers planted outside the front door. Computers were up-to-date and well maintained. The schools were in the city, but they could have been in an affluent suburb, given the attention to detail in the infrastructure.

How had this happened? The inequities were glaring. On one rainy November morning as I was trying to navigate the winding one-way streets of the city, I found myself overwhelmed by my emotions. I pulled my car over to the curb and sat in despair for what seemed like ages. How had some schools received so much, while others had become places that time had forgotten?

The educational policies that made my work as a literacy coach harder weren't all bad. In some ways I understood the beginning of the turnaround process mandated by the Race to the Top program. What I didn't understand was the lack of foresight in how demoralizing the process would be for teachers and administrators and the upheaval it could cause to students and families. I attended "walk-throughs" of schools that had been deemed turnarounds. I attended community meetings informing families of their new options. I sat with teachers to discuss whether or not to reapply for their jobs. I counseled principals about retirement or a new career path. This was a taxing time for all those involved in the process.

Now, it is not that I didn't think something needed to be done. I had worked in many of these schools, saw the needs, and agreed with many of the criticisms of external evaluators. But fire the teachers and hire a whole new team? Was this the answer? How could a school *mindfully* be turned around?

To provide a more effective learning environment in a place that had "failed" to educate all students at an adequate rate of progress was the rationale behind turning around a school—not an ill-intentioned mission, nothing illogical, radical, or misaligned with the values of most educators, myself included. One could argue, "Is it not the responsibility of the public to ensure that students are provided a successful educational experience?" If there were some schools that year after year were not showing signs of progress according to the testing data, was it not our responsibility to do something about it? At the most basic level, the idea of turning a school around made sense to me.

I've since seen that some turnaround strategies really have worked, and not just in the designated "turnaround" schools. When Andy Bott became the principal of the Orchard Gardens K–8 School in Roxbury in 2010, the school was known as a career killer for principals. It had had five principals in its first 7 years. Backpacks were banned for fear that students would store weapons in them. Security guards, costing thousands of dollars, policed the halls. Student performance on state tests was rock-bottom. Teachers assigned to Orchard Gardens asked for transfers or left the profession altogether, creating teacher turnover each year of over 50% of the staff.

How did Andy cope with this situation? He fired all of the security guards and used the money to hire art and music teachers. Restless youth were given clarinets and violins to teach them the discipline required to excel in the performing arts. Funding was raised for paints and easels. Students who did well were given public "shout-outs" over the intercom system each morning, raising morale and confidence.

Orchard Gardens officially turned around, becoming one of the most rapidly improving schools in Boston and in Massachusetts. Student growth increased at 50% or higher each year in English language arts and mathematics in grades 3–8. Celebrities like Yo-Yo Ma visited the school, and students and staff were invited to the White House to meet with President Obama. Policymakers saw Orchard Gardens as a beacon of hope.

Then there are places like the Perry K–8 School, where one of my old student teachers, Geoff Rose, is the principal. Geoff's training prepared him to turn around Perry's results immediately. Still, as a young first-year principal, Geoff knew that he didn't want to go into his school dictating and mandating new initiatives. Yet he knew that there were places for improvement in the school. So he started small and chose a concrete project that would show his staff that by working together, changes could be made. He began with an initiative around reading assessments and resources. The teachers were introduced to an informal reading assessment early in the school year, trained in using it, and supported with the implementation of the tool. Once the administration of the assessment was under way, mindful data analysis of the results became part of the school culture during team meetings and instructional leadership team meetings. Now that the teachers were able to match readers with text using the assessment, a system for housing leveled books was needed. Together with his staff, Geoff ordered the books and organized a space where teachers could easily access leveled texts. The school's English language arts results subsequently improved 71% in a single year.

Not only had Geoff contributed to the academic success of the students in his school, but he had also garnered the respect of his staff. In the spring of his first year, Geoff's faculty wrote a glowing letter of support to the superintendent, endorsing him as a leader and recommending he be given a contract for the upcoming school year. It's important to note that mindful teacher leadership isn't always about overcoming alienated teaching but sometimes about vocal support for good leaders in our schools. Now in his second year as a principal, Geoff has partnered with a local university and two other schools in the neighborhood to implement another initiative around writing.

The Hurley K–8 Dual-Language School in the South End where I now work as an instructional coach is another place where mindful leadership has contributed to student success. Once a level 3 failing school, Hurley is now a level 1 high-performing school that has been recognized by the state as one of the few schools to have substantially narrowed the achievement gap among underrepresented groups. Marjorie Soto, the school's leader, began the process of transitioning the school in 2005, and in September of 2012 Hurley opened for the first time as a Two-Way Immersion (TWI) school. Instead of language being seen as a deficit, it was capitalized on as a strength. Students learn the curriculum for 1 week in English and the next week in Spanish. Parents and community members are welcomed into the school with the message, "Dos Idiomas, Diversas Culturas/Two Languages, Many Cultures."

Teachers at Hurley work together to develop culturally and linguistically responsive curriculum that recognizes that students develop bicultural and biliterate identities over time. Educators attend national dual-language conferences and present their own teacher research at local venues for teachers of second-language learners. These conferences enable others to learn about the innovative work that has been undertaken at Hurley and encourage others to develop dual-language schools.

Marjorie prioritizes the needs of her staff and students when designing professional development. In the spring of 2014 the staff took part in a 3-day whole-school retreat exploring how attitudes and beliefs impact student learning. Recently, after identifying low growth in the special education population, Marjorie gathered a small team of teachers and administrators to brainstorm more effective learning opportunities by presenting case studies in a collaborative manner so that all of us get better at supporting all of our students. Regardless of being a level 1 school, Marjorie and my colleagues are continually seeking ways to improve the practices of the school so that every child succeeds academically and emotionally.

Russell is another school whose leader, Tamara Blake, has fostered mindful teacher leadership to improve student learning through the collaboration with a Boston College professor, Maria Estela Brisk. Dr. Brisk's work focuses on writing strategies for English language learners (ELLs) based on the theory of systemic functional linguistics (SFL). Serving an ELL population of more than 50%, Russell was in need of this type support for its students.

What was unforeseen was the level of professional support this collaboration would provide to the staff of the school. I had worked previously with Dr. Brisk to implement SFL in my 2nd-grade classroom and knew the impact it had on my teaching of writing, which I had struggled with for years. After the first year of working collaboratively with Dr. Brisk and several doctoral students to understand the function of language in texts to develop and implement units of study around reading and writing, the teachers witnessed improved student results on English language arts state assessments. There has been a steady increase on such assessments each year at Russell since its staff began working with Dr. Brisk.

Just as important as improved test scores was the increase in professional learning among the staff at the school. Teachers were now co-teaching language arts courses at Boston College and presenting at national literacy conferences about their work with teaching writing. After district leaders recognized that this professional learning at Russell was contributing to student learning, the SFL work of Maria Brisk expanded to three other schools in Boston. The expertise of the Russell teachers was called upon during a 3-day summer institute introducing the new schools to the theory of teaching writing.

Like Orchard Gardens, Perry, Hurley, and Russell, Trotter Elementary School in Dorchester for years was considered by many to be a lost cause. Student achievement results were at the bottom of the city and state. Crime in the community dominated newspaper headlines. Visionary leadership helped to turn this school around. Principal Mairead Nolan along with Assistant Principal Romaine Mills-Teque have elevated family engagement as an essential foundation of a new collaborative school culture. There has also been an intense focus on curriculum and instruction with a laser-view lens on lesson planning. This includes collaborative planning and weekly review of lessons in a spirit of shared professionalism.

I have been amazed to watch the transformation of Trotter. I had been a district-level literacy coach at the school at the start of Mairead's second year as a principal and witnessed the many challenges she faced. Trotter has become a peaceful school by shifting attention away from demerits and sanctions toward lessons on compassion and values. When I see Trotter today I am reminded of how meaningful the second synergy of creating a loving and caring environment can be for students and teachers.

These exciting stories of schools making real progress have raised my hopes about what could be possible in the BPS in the future. Although it is too soon to tell how everything will roll out, the recently passed Every Student Succeeds Act provides new openings for a less punitive and more decentralized model of education. Boston has a new superintendent, Tommy Chang, who has signaled respect for teachers and our professionalism. The district's Office of Data and Accountability is going beyond simply providing numbers to help educators understand how to make sense of the numbers in ways that can improve instruction. Finally, the district and the commonwealth have reduced the amount of testing in schools. This means not only that students have shorter periods of testing with less frequency throughout the year, but that teachers like my colleagues and I have more time to instruct our students so that they can learn to meet the ambitious goals of the Common Core State Standards. Slowly but surely we are focusing less on accountability and data and more on teaching and learning. The quiet revolution of mindful teaching and learning is part of this exciting new paradigm shift.

NEW WAYS OF THINKING AND LEADING

In each of the cases of mindful school leadership just described, principals worked with their teachers and with the community to transform their schools from outposts of remote testing and accountability policies to centers of teaching and learning. The schools each chose their own unique pathways. Orchard Gardens focused on the arts. Perry's initiative emphasized reading. Hurley developed a dual-language program to capitalize on cultural diversity. Russell collaborated with Boston College to uplift student learning, with a special focus on the writing skills of English language learners. Trotter made team review of lesson planning and community collaboration foundational parts of educational transformation.

We are witnessing the emergence of a new way of thinking about education. BPS Superintendent Chang is emphasizing interdisciplinary team within and across schools. This is a breath of fresh air for educators who have been working in a context that made it seem that new forms of school organization, such as charter or pilot schools, necessarily would lead to innovation in the classrooms. The evolution of a cooperative model, as advocated in our seventh synergy of collective responsibility, slowly is displacing the fear and suspicion promoted by a now anachronistic and discredited change model.

Chang and other BPS leaders are looking beyond student achievement in isolated content areas to explore how students synthesize diverse bodies of knowledge. "The reality is when you're in a job being able to pull information from different sources and integrate them and make sense of it is a critically important skill," Chang has stated. "But we don't practice that way of thinking, because our system doesn't allow for it" (Fitzgerald, 2015, pp. 2–3). Such statements are congruent with the sixth synergy of mindful teaching on integration.

When educators are asked to implement a program or adapt a new curriculum, the animating question must always be a simple one: *What's best for our students?* In some cases, more precision is required, so the question must be: *What's best for our students' learning?* Given the diversity of learners, the answers will vary from case to case. The question should not.

We live on a beautiful planet in a time of increasing abundance, with technological conveniences unimaginable to previous generations. At the same time, climate change and the uneven distribution of wealth threaten all that we have attained and are costing us dearly. A rising generation requires visionary education now more than ever.

Now is the time to stop and to think about what we stand for. Now is the time to renew our professionalism with more mindful approaches to our students, our schools, and our society. Now is the time to recognize that we can never attain what we seek as isolated individuals and that creative and critical collaboration across our profession is imperative if we are to leave a legacy of hope for our students. This is the challenge of mindful teaching and mindful school leadership. It is a challenge we are honored to accept.

Website Information

We hope that you have enjoyed our odyssey into mindful teaching. To learn more about our ongoing activities and to join our online community of inquiry and practice, please visit our website at www.mind fulteacher.com.

References

Abrahamson, E. (2004). *Change without pain*. Cambridge, MA: Harvard Business School Press.

Achinstein, B. (2002). *Community, diversity, and conflict among schoolteachers: The ties that blind*. New York, NY: Teachers College Press.

Alliance for Excellent Education. (2014). *On the path to equity: Improving the effectiveness of beginning teachers*. Washington, DC: Author.

Anyon, J. (2005). *Radical possibilities: Public policy, urban education, and a new social movement*. New York, NY: Routledge.

Austin, J. H. (1999). *Zen and the brain: Toward an understanding of meditation and consciousness*. Cambridge, MA: MIT Press.

Bailey, B. (2000). The impact of mandated change on teachers. In N. Bascia & A. Hargreaves (Eds.), *The sharp edge of educational change: Teaching, leading, and the realities of reform* (pp. 112–128). New York, NY: RoutledgeFalmer.

Begley, S. (2007). *Train your mind, change your brain*. New York, NY: Ballantine.

Benard, B. (2006). Using strength-based practice to tap the resilience of families. In D. Saleebey (Ed.), *Strengths perspective in social work practice* (pp. 197–220). Boston, MA: Allyn & Bacon.

Benedict, R. (1934). *Patterns of culture*. New York, NY: Houghton Mifflin.

Blankstein, A., Houston, P., & Cole, R. (Eds.). (2008). *Sustaining professional learning communities*. Thousand Oaks, CA: Corwin.

Booher-Jennings, J. (2005). Below the bubble: "Educational triage" and the Texas accountability system. *American Educational Research Journal, 42*(2), 231–268.

Brisk, M. E., Dawson, M., Haertgering, M., MacDonald, E., & Zehr, L. (2002). Teaching bilingual students in mainstream classrooms. In Z. Beykont (Ed.), *The power of culture* (pp. 89–120). Cambridge, MA: Harvard Education Publishing Group.

Bryk, A. S., Lee, V. E., & Holland, P. B. (1993). *Catholic schools and the common good*. Cambridge, MA: Harvard University Press.

Bryk, A. S., & Schneider, B. L. (2004). *Trust in schools: A core resource for improvement*. New York, NY: Russell Sage Foundation.

Campbell, E. (2005). Challenges in fostering ethical knowledge as professionalism within schools as teaching communities. *Journal of Educational Change, 6*, 207–226.

Carr, N. (2010). *The shallows: What the Internet is doing to our brains.* New York, NY: W.W. Norton.

Celio, M. B., & Harvey, J. (2005). *Buried treasure: Developing an effective management guide from mountains of educational data.* Seattle, WA: Center on Reinventing Public Education.

Chapman, C., & Muijs, D. (2013). Does school-to-school collaboration promote school improvement? A study of the impact of school federations on student outcomes. *School Effectiveness and School Improvement, 6*(39), 351–393.

Chen, E., Heritage, M., & Lee, J. (2005). Identifying and monitoring students' learning needs with technology. *Journal of Education for Students Placed at Risk, 10*(3), 309–332.

Cochran-Smith, M., & Lytle, S. L. (1993). *Inside/outside: Teacher research and knowledge.* New York, NY: Teachers College Press.

Cochran-Smith, M., & Lytle, S. L. (2009). *Inquiry as stance: Practitioner research in the next generation.* New York, NY: Teachers College Press.

Cohen, D. K. (1990). A revolution in one classroom: The case of Mrs. Oublier. *Educational evaluation and policy analysis, 12*(3), 327–345.

Conway, J. M., & Andrews, D. (2015). A school wide approach to leading pedagogical enhancement: An Australian perspective. *Journal of Educational Change, 17*(1), 115–139.

Cooper, K. S., Stanulis, R. N., Brondyk, S. K., Hamilton, E. R., Macaluso, M., & Meier, J. A. (2015). The teacher leadership process: Attempting change within embedded systems. *Journal of Educational Change, 17*(1), 85–113.

Council of Great City Schools. (2014). Urban school superintendents: Characteristics, tenure, and salary. Eighth survey and report. *Urban Indicator.* Retrieved from www.cgcs.org/cms/lib/DC00001581/Centricity/Domain/87/Urban%20Indicator_Superintendent%20Summary%2011514.pdf

Craig, C. (2006). Why is dissemination so difficult? The nature of teacher knowledge and the spread of curriculum reform. *American Education Research Journal, 43*(2), 257–293.

Cripe, F. (1986). Rock music as therapy for children with attention deficit disorder: An exploratory study. *Journal of Music Therapy, 23*(1), 30–37.

Cusick, P. A. (2002). *A study of Michigan's principal shortage.* East Lansing, MI: Education Policy Center, Michigan State University.

Daly, A. (Ed.). (2010). *Social network theory and educational change.* Cambridge, MA: Harvard Education Press.

Darling-Hammond, L. (1990). Instructional policy into practice: "The power of the bottom over the top." *Educational Evaluation and Policy Analysis, 12*(3), 339–347.

Dewey, J. (1916). *Democracy and education*. New York, NY: Free Press.

Dewey, J. (1938). *Experience and education*. New York, NY: Collier.

Dynarski, M. (2008). Researchers and educators: Allies in learning. *Phi Delta Kappan, 66*(4), 48–53.

Emo, W. (2015). Teachers' motivations for initiating innovations. *Journal of Educational Change, 16*(2), 171–196.

Evans, R. (2001). *The human side of school change: Reform, resistance, and the real-life problems of innovation*. San Francisco, CA: Jossey-Bass.

Fitzgerald, M. (2015) Tommy Chang on leading a school system like a startup. *Boston Globe*. Retrieved from https://www.bostonglobe.com/magazine/2015/10/01/tommy-chang-leading-school-system-like-startup/faMr3x3exk8G2FxNcArRWP/story.html

Formisano, R. P. (1991). *Boston against busing: Race, class, and ethnicity in the 1960s and 1970s*. Chapel Hill, NC: University of North Carolina Press.

Freire, P. (2000). *Pedagogy of the oppressed*. New York: Continuum.

Fried, R. L. (1995). *The passionate teacher: A practical guide*. Boston, MA: Beacon Press.

Friedman, A. (2004). Beyond mediocrity: Transformational leadership within a transactional framework. *International Journal of Leadership in Education, 7*(3), 203–224.

Frisina, W. G. (2002). *The unity of knowledge and action: Toward a nonrepresentational theory of knowledge*. Albany, NY: State University of New York Press.

Fullan, M. (2001). *The new meaning of educational change*. New York, NY: Teachers College Press.

Fullan, M. (2008). *The six secrets of change: What the best leaders do to help their organizations survive and thrive*. San Francisco: Jossey-Bass.

Gardner, H., Csikszentmihalyi, M., & Damon, W. (2001). *Good work: When excellence and ethics meet*. New York, NY: Basic Books.

Gee, J. P. (2007). *What video games have to teach us about learning and literacy*. New York, NY: Palgrave MacMillan.

Gil, E. (2006). *Helping abused and traumatized children: Integrating directive and nondirective approaches*. New York: Guilford Press.

Hamilton, L. S., Stecher, B. M., Marsh, J. A., McCombs, J. S., Robyn, A., Russell, J. L., . . . Barney, H. (2007). *Standards-based accountability under No Child Left Behind: Experiences of teachers and administrators in three states*. Santa Monica, CA: RAND.

Hanh, T. N. (1988). *The heart of understanding*. Berkeley, CA: Parallax Press.

Hanh, T. N. (1992). *The diamond that cuts through illusion*. Berkeley, CA: Parallax Press.

Hanh, T. N. (1998). *Interbeing: Fourteen guidelines for engaged Buddhism*. Berkeley, CA: Parallax Press.

Hanh, T. N. (2005). *Keeping the peace: Mindfulness and public service*. Berkeley, CA: Parallax Press.

Hargreaves, A. (1994). *Changing teachers, changing times: Teachers work and culture in the postmodern age.* New York, NY: Teachers College Press.

Hargreaves, A. (2003). *Teaching in the knowledge society: Education in the age of insecurity.* New York, NY: Teachers College Press.

Hargreaves, A. (2004). Inclusive and exclusive educational change: Emotional responses of teachers and implications for leadership. In *School Leadership and Management, 24*(2), 287–309.

Hargraves, A., Boyle, A., & Harris, A. (2014). *Uplifting leadership: How organizations, teams, and communities raise performance.* San Francisco: Jossey-Bass.

Hargreaves, A., & Braun, H. (2012). *Leading for all.* Toronto, Canada: Council of Ontario Directors of Education.

Hargreaves, A., & Fink, D. (2006). *Sustainable leadership.* San Francisco, CA: Jossey-Bass.

Hargreaves, A., & Fullan, M. (2012). *Professional capital: Transforming teaching in every school.* New York, NY: Teachers College Press.

Hargreaves, A., Halász, G., & Pont, B. (2008). The Finnish approach to system leadership. In B. Pont, D. Nusche, & D. Hopkins (Eds.), *Improving school leadership. Vol. 2: Case studies on system leadership* (pp. 69–109). Paris, France: OECD.

Hargreaves, A., & Shirley, D. (2008). Beyond standardization: Powerful new principles for improvement. *Phi Delta Kappan, 90*(2), 135–143.

Hargreaves, A., & Shirley, D. (2009a). The persistence of presentism. *Teachers College Record, 111*(11), 2505–2534.

Hargreaves, A., & Shirley, D. (2009b). *The fourth way: The inspiring future of educational change.* Thousand Oaks, CA: Corwin.

Hargreaves, A., & Shirley, D. (2012). *The global fourth way: The quest for educational excellence.* Thousand Oaks, CA: Corwin.

Hargreaves, A., Shirley, D., Evans, M., Stone-Johnson, C., & Riseman, D. (2007). *The long and short of school improvement: Final evaluation of the Raising Achievement Transforming Learning Programme of the Specialist Schools and Academies Trust.* London, England: Specialist Schools and Academies Trust.

Harris, A. (2008). *Distributed school leadership: Developing tomorrow's leaders.* London, England: Routledge.

Henry, G., Fortner, K., & Bastian, K. (2012). The effects of experience and attrition for novice high school science and mathematics teachers. *Science, 335*, 1118–1121.

Hewitt, P., Pijanowski, J., Carnine, L., & Denny, G. (2008). *The status of school leadership in Arkansas.* Fayetteville, AR: University of Arkansas.

Hopkins, D. (2001). *School improvement for real.* New York, NY: RoutledgeFalmer.

Hopmann, S. (2007). Restrained teaching: The common core of Didaktik. *European Educational Research Journal, 6*(2), 109–124.

Horn, M. B., & Staker, H. (2015). *Blended: Using disruptive innovation to improve schools.* San Francisco, CA: Jossey-Bass.

Huberman, M. (1993). *The lives of teachers.* New York, NY: Teachers College Press.

Huberman, M. (1999). The mind is its own place: The influence of sustained interactivity with practitioners on educational researchers. *Harvard Educational Review, 69*(3), 289–319.

Ingersoll, R. M. (2003). *Who controls teachers' work? Power and accountability in America's schools.* Cambridge, MA: Harvard University Press.

Ingersoll, R. M., Merrill, L., & Stuckey, D. (2014) *Seven trends: The transformation of the teaching force.* Philadelphia: CPRE Research Reports.

Ingram, D., Seashore Louis, K., & Schroeder, R. G. (2004). Accountability policies and teacher decision making: Barriers to the use of data to improve practice. *Teachers College Record, 106*(6), 1258–1287.

Ito, M. (Ed.). (2010). *Hanging out, messing around, and geeking out: Kids living and learning with the new media.* Cambridge, MA: MIT Press.

Jenkins, H., Clinton, K., Purushotma, R., Robison, A. J., & Weigel, M. (2006). *Confronting the challenges of participatory culture: Media education for the 21st century.* Chicago, IL: MacArthur Foundation.

Kellerman, B. (2012). *The end of leadership.* New York: Harper Business.

King, P. M., & Kitchener, K. S. (1994). *Developing reflective judgment: Understanding and promoting intellectual growth and critical thinking in adolescents and adults.* San Francisco, CA: Jossey-Bass.

Klafki, W. (1994). *Neue Studien zur Bildungstheorie und Didaktik: Zeitgemäße Allgemeinbildung und kritsch-konstruktive Didaktik.* [New Studies on Educational Theory and Didactics: Contemporary General Education and Critical-Constructive Didactics.] Weinheim, Germany: Beltz.

Klafki, W. (2000). Didaktik analysis as the core of preparation of instruction. In I. Westbury, S. Hopmann, & K. Riquarts (Eds.), *Teaching as a reflective practice: The German Didaktik tradition* (pp. 139–159). Mahwah, NJ: Erlbaum. Original work published 1958.

Klingberg, L. (1990). *Lehrende und Lernende im Unterricht: Zur didaktischen Aspekten ihrer Positionen im Unterrichtsprozeß.* [Teaching and Learning in Instruction: Towards Didactic Aspects of their Roles in the Process of Instruction.] Berlin, Germany: Volk und Wissen.

Labaree, D. F. (2004). *The trouble with ed schools.* New Haven: Yale University Press.

Lagemann, E. C. (2002). *An elusive science: The troubling history of education research.* Chicago: University of Chicago Press.

Lane, R. E. (2000). *The loss of happiness in market democracies.* New Haven, CT: Yale University Press.

Langer, E. J. (1989). *Mindfulness.* Reading, MA: Addison-Wesley.

Langer, E. J. (1997). *The power of mindful learning.* Reading, MA: Addison-Wesley.

Lantieri, L. (2008). *Building emotional intelligence.* Boulder, CO: Sounds True.

Leithwood, K., Jantzi, D., & Steinbach, R. (1999). *Changing leadership for changing times.* Buckingham, England: Open University Press.

Lieberman, A., & Miller, L. (2004). *Teacher leadership.* San Francisco, CA: Jossey-Bass.

Lieberman, A., & Miller, L. (Eds.). (2008). *Teachers in professional communities: Improving teaching and learning.* New York, NY: Teachers College Press.

Lieberman, A., & Wood, D. R. (2003). *Inside the National Writing Project: Connecting network learning and classroom teaching.* New York, NY: Teachers College Press.

Lima, J. A. (2001). Forgetting about friendship: Using conflict in teacher communities as a catalyst for school change. *Journal of Educational Change, 2,* 97–122.

Liston, D., Whitcomb, J., & Borko, H. (2007) NCLB and scientifically-based research: Opportunities lost and found. *Journal of Teacher Education 58*(2), 99–107.

Liston, D. P., & Zeichner, K. M. (1990). Reflective teaching and action research in preservice teacher education. *Journal of Education for Teaching, 16*(3), 235–254.

Little, J.W., & Bartlett, L. (2002) Career and commitment in the context of comprehensive school reform. *Theory and Practice,* 8(3), 345–354.

Lortie, D. (1975). *Schoolteacher: A sociological study.* Chicago, IL: University of Chicago Press.

Marx, K. (1978). Economic and philosophical manuscripts. In R. C. Tucker (Ed.), *The Marx-Engels Reader* (pp. 66–125). New York, NY: Norton. Original work published 1844.

Maathai, W. (2007). Unbowed: A memoir. New York: Anchor.

Maslow, A. H. (1969). *The psychology of science: A reconnaissance.* Chicago, IL: Gateway.

McDonald, J. P., Mohr, N., Dichter, A., & McDonald, E. (2007). *The power of protocols: An educator's guide to better practice.* New York, NY: Teachers College Press.

McLaughlin, M. W. (2006). Implementation research in education: Lessons learned, lingering questions and new opportunities. In M. I. Honig (Ed.), *New directions in education policy implementation: Confronting complexity* (pp. 209–228). Albany, NY: State University of New York Press.

McLaughlin, M. W., & Talbert, J. (2001). *Professional communities and the work of high school teaching.* Chicago, IL: University of Chicago Press.

McQuillan, P. J. (1998). *Educational opportunity in an urban American high school: A cultural analysis.* Albany, NY: State University of New York Press.

Mill, J. S. (1867). Inaugural address delivered to the university at St. Andrews. London: Longmans, Green, Reader, & Dryer.

Miller, L. (2015). *The spiritual child: The new science on parenting for health and lifelong thriving.* New York: St. Martin's Press.

Montgomery, K. C. (2007). *Generation digital: Politics, commerce, and childhood in the age of the Internet.* Cambridge: MIT Press.

Moore Johnson, S., Marietta, G., Higgins, M. C., Mapp, K. L., & Grossman, A. (2015). *Achieving coherence in district improvement: Managing the relationship between central office and schools.* Cambridge, MA: Harvard Education Press.

Murphy, J., Goldring, E., & Porter, A. (2006). *Leadership for learning: A research-based model and taxonomy of behaviors.* Paper presented at the Wallace Foundation State Action for Educational Leadership Conference, Saint Louis, MO.

Murrell, P. C., Jr. (2001). *The community teacher: A new framework for effective urban teaching.* New York, NY: Teachers College Press.

Newmann, F., & Wehlage, G. (1995). *Successful school restructuring.* Madison, WI: Center on Organization and Restructuring of Schools.

Nielsen Company. (2010). U.S. teen mobile report: Calling yesterday, texting today, using apps tomorrow. *Nielsen News.* Retrieved from www .nielsen.com/us/en/insights/news/2010/u-s-teen-mobile-report-calling-yesterday-texting-today-using-apps-tomorrow.html

Nieto, S. (2003). *What keeps teachers going?* New York, NY: Teachers College Press.

Noddings, N. (1992). *The challenge to care in schools.* New York, NY: Teachers College Press.

Noddings, N. (2001). Care and coercion in school reform. *Journal of Educational Change, 2,* 35–43.

Noguera, P. A. (2008). *The trouble with black boys . . . and other reflections on race, equity, and the future of public education.* San Francisco, CA: Jossey-Bass.

Oakes, J., Rogers, J., & Lipton, M. (2006). *Learning power: Organizing for education and justice.* New York, NY: Teachers College Press.

O'Connor, M. T. (forthcoming). Investigating students' language choices in response to audience in argument writing lessons in rural secondary classrooms. *Journal of Literacy Research.*

Ogilby, H. (2007). Teacher leadership: Noble aspiration or myth? In R. H. Ackerman & S. V. Mackenzie (Eds.), *Uncovering teacher leadership* (pp. 161–166). Thousand Oaks, CA: Corwin Press.

Ontario Ministry of Education. (2014). Achieving excellence: A renewed vision for education in Ontario. Toronto: Ontario Ministry of Education.

Palfrey, J., & Gasser, U. (2008). *Born digital: Understanding the first generation of digital natives.* New York, NY: Basic Books.

Pallotta, F. (2004). *Freedom is an endless meeting: Democracy in American social movements.* Chicago, IL: University of Chicago Press.

Palmer, P. J. (1998). *The courage to teach: Exploring the inner landscape of a teacher's life.* San Francisco, CA: Jossey-Bass.

Payne, C. M. (2008). *So much reform, so little change.* Cambridge, MA: Harvard Education Press.

Payton, J., Weissberg, R. P., Durlak, J. A., Dymnicki, A. B., Taylor, R. D., Schellinger, K. B., & Pachan, M. (2008). *The positive impact of social and emotional learning for kindergarten to eighth-grade students: Findings from three scientific reviews.* Chicago, IL: Collaborative for Academic, Social, and Emotional Learning.

Pedulla, J., Abrams, L. M., Madaus, G. F., Russell, M. K., Ramos, M. A., & Miao, J. (2003). *Perceived effects of state-mandated testing programs on teaching and learning: Findings from a national survey of teachers.* Chestnut Hill, MA: National Board on Educational Testing and Public Policy.

Perda, D. (2013). *Transitions into and out of teaching: A longitudinal analysis of early career teacher turnover* (Unpublished doctoral dissertation). University of Pennsylvania, Philadelphia, PA.

Perlstein, D. H. (2004). *Justice, justice: School politics and the eclipse of liberalism.* New York, NY: Peter Lang.

Peterman, F. P. (Ed.). (2008). *Partnering to prepare urban teachers: A call to activism.* New York, NY: Peter Lang.

Piketty, T. (2014). *Capital in the twenty-first century.* Cambridge, MA: Harvard University Press.

Pope Francis. (2015). *Laudatio si: On care for our common home.* Vatican City: Libreria Editrice Vaticana.

Pressman, J. L., & Wildavsky, A. (1973). *Implementation: How great expectations in Washington are dashed in Oakland.* Berkeley, CA: University of California Press.

Ramsburg, J. T., & Youmans, R. J. (2013). Meditation in the higher education classroom: Meditation training improves student knowledge retention during lectures. *Mindfulness, 5*(4), 431–441. doi:10.1007/s12671-013-0199-5

Ravitch, D. (2000). *Left back: A century of failed school reform.* New York, NY: Simon & Schuster.

Rechtschaffen, D. (2014). *The way of mindful education: Cultivating well-being in teachers and students.* New York, NY: W.W. Norton.

Reville, S. P. (Ed.). (2007). *A decade of urban school reform: Persistence and progress in the Boston public schools.* Cambridge, MA: Harvard Education Press.

Rincón-Gallardo, S. (2015). Bringing a counter-hegemonic pedagogy to scale in Mexican public schools. *Multidisciplinary Journal of Educational Research, 5*(1), 28–54.

Rosen, L. D. (2011). Teaching the iGeneration. *Educational Leadership, 68*(5), 10–15.

Rosenholtz, S. (1989). *Teachers' workplace.* New York, NY: Longman.

Sahlberg, P. (2015). *Finnish lessons 2.0: What can the world learn from educational change in Finland?* New York, NY: Teachers College Press.

Scheurich, J. J. (1998). Highly successful and loving, public elementary schools populated mainly by low-SES children of color: Core beliefs and cultural characteristics. *Urban Education, 33*(4), 451–491.

Schleiermacher, F. (2000). *Texte zur Pädagogik* (Vol. 2). Frankfurt, Germany: Suhrkamp. Original work published 1826.

Schön, D. A. (1987). *Educating the reflective practitioner: Toward a new design for teaching and learning in the professions.* San Francisco, CA: Jossey-Bass.

Seligman, M. E. P. (2002). *Authentic happiness.* New York, NY: Free Press.

Selman, M. (1988). Schoen's gate is square: But is it art? In P. P. Grimmett & G. I. Erickson (Eds.), *Reflection in teacher education* (pp. 177–192). New York, NY: Teachers College Press.

Senge, P., Smith, B., Kruschwitz, N., Laur, J., & Schley, S. (2008). *The necessary revolution: How individuals and organizations are working together to create a sustainable world.* New York, NY: Doubleday.

Shirley, D. (1997). *Community organizing for urban school reform.* Austin, TX: University of Texas Press.

Shirley, D. (2002). *Valley Interfaith and school reform: Organizing for power in South Texas.* Austin, TX: University of Texas Press.

Shirley, D. (2006a). Street-level democrats: Realizing the potential of school, university, and community coalitions. *Educational Forum, 70*(2), 116–122.

Shirley, D. (2006b). The Massachusetts Coalition for Teacher Quality and Student Achievement: An introduction. *Excellence and Equity in Education, 39*(1), 4–14.

Shirley, D. (2008a). The coming of post-standardization in education: What role for the German Didaktik tradition? *Zeitschrift für Erziehungswissenschaft, 10*(9), 35–46.

Shirley, D. (2008b). American perspectives on German educational theory and research: A closer look at both the American educational context and the German Didaktik tradition. In K. H. Arnold, S. Blömeke, R. Messner, & J. Schlömerkemper (Eds.), *Allgemeine Didaktik und Lehr-Lernforschung: Kontrontroversen und Entwicklungsperspektiven einer Wissenschaft von Unterricht.* [General didactics and research on teaching and learning: Controversies and developmental perspectives on a science of instruction.] Paderborn, Germany: Klinckhardt, 195–210.

Shirley, D., & Hargreaves, A. (2006). Data-driven to distraction. *Education Week, 26*(4), 32–33.

Shirley, D., Hersi, A., MacDonald, E., Sanchez, M. T., Scandone, C., Skidmore, C., & Tutwiler, P. (2006). Bringing the community back in: Change, accommodation, and contestation in a school and university partnership. *Excellence and Equity in Education, 39*(1), 27–36.

Siegel, D. J. (2007). *The mindful brain: Reflection and attunement in the cultivation of well-being.* New York, NY: Norton.

Sisodia, R. S., Wolfe, D. B., & Sheth, J. N. (2007). *Firms of endearment: How world-class companies profit from passion and purpose.* Upper Saddle River, NJ: Wharton School Publishing.

Small, G., & Vorgan, G. (2009). *iBrain: Surviving the technological alteration of the modern mind.* New York: William Morrow.

Snow, C., Burns, M. S., & Griffin, P. (1998). *Preventing reading difficulties in young children.* Washington, DC: National Academy Press.

Soros, G. (2008). *The new paradigm for financial markets.* New York, NY: PublicAffairs.

Spillane, J. P. (2006). *Distributed leadership.* San Francisco, CA: Jossey-Bass.

Spillane, J. P., & Diamond, J. B. (2007). Taking a distributed perspective. In J. P. Spillane & J. B. Diamond (Eds.), *Distributed leadership in practice* (pp. 1–15). New York, NY: Teachers College Press.

Stoll, L., Bolgam, R., McMahon, A., Wallace, M., & Thomas, S. (2006). Professional learning communities: A review of the literature. *Journal of Educational Change, 7*(4), 221–258.

Stoll, L., & Louis, K. S. (Eds.). (2007). *Professional learning communities: Divergence, depth and dilemmas.* Berkshire, England: Open University Press.

Stone-Johnson, C. (2015). Intensification and isolation: Alienated teaching and collaborative professional relationships in the accountability context. *Journal of Educational Change, 17*(1), 29–49.

Symonds, K. W. (2003). *After the test: How schools are using data to close the achievement gap.* San Francisco, CA: Bay Area School Reform Collaborative.

Taleb, N. N. (2007). *The black swan: The impact of the highly improbable.* New York: Random House.

Torres, A. S. (2012). "Hello, goodbye": Exploring the phenomenon of leaving teaching early. *Journal of Educational Change, 13*(1), 117–154.

Trilling, B., & Fadel, C. (2009). *21st century skills: Learning for life in our times.* New York, NY: Basic Books.

Turkle, S. (2011). *Alone together: Why we expect more from technology and less from each other.* New York, NY: Basic Books.

Turkle, S. (2015). *Reclaiming conversation: The power of talk in a digital age.* New York, NY: Penguin.

Tyler, R. W. (1949). *Basic principles of curriculum and instruction.* Chicago, IL: University of Chicago Press.

Tyler, R. W. (1993). The Tyler rationale reconsidered. In G. Willis, W. H. Schubert, R. V. Bullough, C. Kridel, & J. T. Holton (Eds.), *The American curriculum: A documentary history* (pp. 395–400). Westwood, CT: Praeger. Original work published 1977.

UNESCO. (2013). *Child well-being in rich countries: A comparative overview.* Florence, Italy: Innocenti Center.

Wagner, T., & Dintersmith, T. (2015). *Most likely to succeed: Preparing our kids for the innovation era.* New York, NY: Scribner.

Wells, C. M., & Feun, L. (2013). Educational change and professional learning communities: A study of two districts. *Journal of Educational Change, 14*(2), 233–257.

Welner, K. G. (2001). *Legal rights, local wrongs: When community control collides with educational equity.* Albany, NY: State University of New York Press.

Westbury, I., Hopmann, S., & Riquarts, K. (2000). *Teaching as a reflective practice: The German Didaktik tradition.* Mahwah, NJ: Lawrence Erlbaum.

Yellup, A. (2013). Making sure every person matters. In D. Crossley (Ed.), *Sustainable school transformation: An inside-out school led approach* (pp. 253–276). London, England: Bloomsbury.

Index

Page references followed by the letter *f* refer to figures.

About the Authors

Dennis Shirley is a professor of education at the Lynch School of Education at Boston College. He is the editor in chief of the *Journal of Educational Change* and author of *The New Imperatives of Educational Change: Achievement with Integrity*.

Elizabeth MacDonald is an educator and instructional coach in the Boston Public Schools.

Dennis and Liz have presented their research at professional development conferences in many countries and throughout the United States. For more information, visit www.mindfulteacher.com.